Freedom

M A **THRIVE**MOMS
BIBLE STUDY

Freedom

LETTING GO AND
EMBRACING CHRIST

Kara-Kae James
& Ali Pedersen

DAVID C COOK
transforming lives together

FREEDOM
Published by David C Cook
4050 Lee Vance Drive
Colorado Springs, CO 80918 U.S.A.

Integrity Music Limited, a Division of David C Cook
Brighton, East Sussex BN1 2RE, England

The website addresses recommended throughout this book are offered as a resource to you. These websites are not intended in any way to be or imply an endorsement on the part of David C Cook, nor do we vouch for their content.

All Scripture quotations are taken from the Christian Standard Bible®, Copyright © 2017 by Holman Bible Publishers. Used by permission. Christian Standard Bible® and CSB® are federally registered trademarks of Holman Bible Publishers. The authors have added italic and bold treatment to Scripture quotations for emphasis.

ISBN 978-0-8307-7310-7
eISBN 978-0-8307-7913-0

© 2019 Kara-Kae James
The Author is represented by Alive Literary Agency, 7680 Goddard Street, Suite 200, Colorado Springs, CO 80920, www.aliveliterary.com.

Cowritten by Ali Pedersen
The Team: Alice Crider, Laura Derico, Amy Konyndyk, Nick Lee, Jack Campbell, Susan Murdock
Cover Design: Jon Middel

Printed in the United States of America
First Edition 2019

1 2 3 4 5 6 7 8 9 10

061919

CONTENTS

HOW TO USE THIS STUDY

Before you get going, pause a sec: What do you hope to get out of this study? (Write your answer below.)

Welcome to this Thrive Moms Bible study! Thrive Moms (www.thrivemoms.com) is a ministry that exists to encourage and inspire moms everywhere to do more than just *survive* motherhood. We want you to thrive, and we believe thriving happens when you connect with God's Word and one another.

This Bible study can be done as an individual or with a group. But we know we are always better together! Even if you grab just one friend to walk through the study with you, you'll stay on track better and keep each other accountable.

There are six weeks of study, and each week has four days (to not overwhelm you). Do these day studies at the times that work best for you. Each study week includes these features:

- Go to the Word sections to offer specific Bible verses to focus on.
- Simple questions to help you process the Bible passages.
- Space provided for you to make your own connections.

- Prayer suggestions to lead into your personal time with God.

Each week wraps up with a group discussion option, designed to offer time to talk over what you've learned from God's Word through the week, to share your experiences, and to learn from and encourage one another.

Prepare yourself with time and accountability as you begin. We are cheering you on into freedom as you study!

GROUP DISCUSSION GROUND RULES

SAFE SPACE

You are entering a safe space here, and it will all be worth it. Allow yourself to break down some walls and trust the women God has placed around you. Be honest and trustworthy with others. A key part of your personal growth is found in community with others. Be intentional in your conversation and the way you process Scripture.

COMMITMENT

Commit to do the work! We have made the study sessions intentionally short so that they are not overly time consuming. (They were written for busy moms!) Whether you are doing the study on your own, with a friend, or with a group, make the commitment to attend and be involved. You'll get the most out of this study if you commit to it. The curriculum is not overwhelming, so there are no excuses!

DISCUSSION

When talking in a group, be concise with your answers. Remember that everyone's time is precious, and everyone should have an opportunity to speak. What happens in the group, stays in the group. Keep discussion confidential. Scripture is our basis for everything. We may be drawn to giving worldly advice, but the best truth is God's!

If you are leading a group, see more tips for leaders at the end of this book in the Leader Guide.

WHY FREEDOM?

I'm sure many of us have seen the movie *Braveheart* (or at least heard it on in the background as our husbands watch it for the four millionth time) and heard the passionate battle cry of William Wallace. *"They may take our lives, but they'll never take ... our freedom!"* Christians can boast a similar claim! We may not paint our faces blue or march into a literal battle, but we are guaranteed a freedom that no one can take from us. We are not bound by this world. It has no claim on us. We belong to Christ, and as His children, we enjoy a freedom like no other.

Although most of us live fundamentally free lives, as moms we can so often feel bound by cultural norms, expectations from friends or family, and more. A battle for our minds and hearts is happening. The enemy is at work! He wants us to feel suffocated by our lives and to rob us of experiencing the joy of motherhood and the gift of this life and the next.

But there's an answer. There's hope on the days when we feel suffocated by our expectations, our guilt, and our pressure to do it all. There's freedom offered to us (yes, even you, tired and weary mom!) in the midst of the battles we face. There's a hand reaching out to grab us off the battlefield, and One who prepares a feast for us in the midst of our enemies.

The freedom that Jesus offers from the tugs and burdens of this world makes the journey well worth it. It gives us something beautiful to offer to our children as we battle on together. Freedom is here for you, friend. It's yours for the taking. It's not something you have to fight for or work harder for; Jesus did all that on the cross.

It's time to throw off the fear, shame, expectations, guilt, and judgment, and run in the freedom that Christ offers. It's time to let go and embrace all that He has, so you can live freely.

Let's not allow the enemy to succeed! Let's take back our motherhood! Let's take back our freedom! This is our battle cry! Are you with us?

WHAT IS FREEDOM IN CHRIST?

I'll be honest—I was a terrible history student when I was growing up. I was bored with the subject matter. I mean, come on—the past is the past, right? I was completely clueless when it came to US history, world history, and even biblical history. But as I became an adult, things started to change. I realized the world was so much bigger than me and my Western privilege, and there was a great big world to learn from out there. I started learning about history and how it has shaped us, and what freedom has meant for different people throughout the centuries. My eyes were opened, and it has since transformed the way I live and approach everything I do.

Freedom to me always seemed like a no-brainer. I'm free because that's my life, my economic standard, my political status. But that's not the case for everyone. Most of us don't even have to think about our freedom; it's just something that we've always had—like our mother's eyes or our father's quirky laugh. Persecution is not part of our daily existence. For example, I would guess you have easy access to a Bible and may even have multiple copies around your house.

We feel free—that's enough, right?

Sometimes, because of our everyday reality, we tend to overlook what it means to be free as followers of Jesus. But I want to encourage us to shift our thinking from political, financial, or even religious freedom, to a different kind of freedom. *Freedom in Christ.* That's what we'll spend the next week diving deeper into as we read through the book of Galatians.

Day One

NO OTHER GOSPEL
Galatians 1

We kick off this week in a bit of a rough patch. One of our favorite apostles, Paul, is a little ticked off. It's like when your child "accidently" throws your favorite tube of lipstick in the washing machine just for fun and then laughs in the corner as you cry in the laundry basket of ruined clothes a few days later.

Things just aren't good around Galatia, and Paul is extremely disappointed in the churches there. The tone he takes with these believers in his letter implies that he knows them well and has a deep relationship with them. I've read suggestions in some commentaries that say Paul might have taken the pen from his scribe and written the end of the letter himself. Probably in all caps, just to drive the point home ("Look at what large letters I use," Galatians 6:11).

Go to the Word: *Read Galatians 1.1–5.*

How does Paul describe himself?

To whom is Paul writing?

If we compare and contrast almost all of Paul's letters against this letter, we find a difference right at the beginning. (For example, see 1 Corinthians, Ephesians, Philippians, and Colossians.) Don't be too quick to skip over the greetings of his letters—they can tell us a lot. "Grace and peace" is how he typically begins, and then he gives an offering of thanksgiving. But not here.

Paul jumps right from grace and peace into frustration: "I am amazed that you are so quickly turning away from him who called you by the grace of Christ and are turning to a different gospel" (Galatians 1:6).

Ouch.

I shared in my book *Mom Up* how some people in our lives have "refrigerator rights." These are the people we have deep personal relationships with, who can literally walk into our homes and feel comfortable enough to help themselves to the fridge, and we can do the same in their homes. We don't only have rights to their food, coffeemaker, and best chocolate stash—we have rights to personally provoke and encourage them.

Hebrews 10:24-25 reads: "And let us watch out for one another to provoke love and good works, not neglecting to gather together, as some are in the habit of doing, but encouraging each other." The word *provoke* may sound negative at first, but the idea here is to call out and challenge the people who are walking through life with us, and to encourage them when they are struggling. Our refrigerator friends have earned the right to speak into our lives this way, and this is how we help each other grow. When one of my close friends sees me slipping, she has the right to provoke me.

Paul had this kind of relationship with the Galatians. He was calling them out on their slipping, continuing to push them away from the false gospel they had started to follow.

Paul uses phrases like "the gospel of Christ" and the "truth of the gospel" throughout this letter. Imagine you were explaining what the gospel means to a child. How would you describe it to them?

✐ Go to the Word: *Read Galatians 1:3–5. Look at the way Paul breaks it down: What does he tell us about Jesus in these verses?*

Verse 3:

Verse 4:

Verse 5:

✐ Go to the Word: *Read Galatians 1:6–10.*

This letter to the Galatians is all about the gospel, and in ways we might find that a bit surprising, because Paul was writing to Christians who already believed in the gospel.

Based on what you've learned about the Galatians, why do you think it was so important for Paul to emphasize his message about the gospel?

Something we often forget—because it's always right in front of us—is that we need the gospel just as much as non-believers need the gospel. We lose our way sometimes, we forget our journey, and we take our eyes off the destination ahead. We (often like children) need constant reminding of the gospel of Christ and the freedom that can be found in it.

How do we "distort the gospel" (Galatians 1:7) today in ways that may take away from the power of the gospel message?

What is Paul's attitude toward people who distort the gospel?

PRAYER FOR FREEDOM

Pray with Paul, thanking Christ for rescuing us and freeing us from this present evil age. Ask God to remind you to stay close to the gospel of Christ.

Day Two

THE LAW AND THE PROMISE
Galatians 2:11–21; 3:1–29

I majored in journalism in college, and one course I had to take was media law. A lot of journalism students hated this course, mostly because the professor was really tough, but also because it was nothing like our normal docket of coursework. This class was all about learning a specific set of rules and guidelines that writers must follow when writing for media.

And me? I'm a type A, Enneagram-one rule follower. So ... I LOVED it. Learning the rules and how they fit together made sense to me, and I enjoyed the hours I had to spend memorizing each and every law that we bright-eyed, young journalists and PR professionals needed to know to step into our careers ethically and lawfully. That one class almost made me want to go to law school just because I'm that much of a rule follower.

Still to this day I love a good set of rules and margin. Rules make sense to me and help me feel at ease and able to accomplish what I need to do without distraction. So, as you might guess, I can sympathize with the Galatians a bit when we read about them falling back into the ancient Law.

You see, the ancient Law (prior to Christ's resurrection) was put in place to give people a way back to God. They could follow a set of rules, and this would put them in right standing with God. But Paul points out that Christ turned this idea on its head.

✍ **Go to the Word:** *Read Galatians 2:11–21.*

What does Paul say will not happen by the works of the Law?

What does he claim would be true if righteousness came through the Law?

✐ **Go to the Word:** *Read Galatians 3.*

Paul goes on to explain to the Galatians, in chapter 3, how Jesus changed everything! When Jesus died, He fulfilled the Law and made it obsolete! Rather than people needing to fulfill the Law in order to be saved, they only needed to place their faith in Jesus. Faith—not the Law—was the great gift here.

Let's pretend that Paul is a lawyer in this scenario, now that I'm reminiscing on my law study days, and look a little deeper at this text. In Galatians 3, what are five reasons Paul presents to the Galatians for understanding why salvation comes by faith and not by the Law?

1.

2.

3.

4.

5.

"You foolish Galatians!" Paul calls his friends out yet again here in chapter 3. Not exactly a compliment. He wasn't implying that they were just frivolous, innocent, or uneducated. The Greek word Paul used for "foolish" was *anoetos*,[1] meaning that they had been taught but were choosing not to use the power of their minds. Roughly translated, now this would probably read more like "Come on, you senseless idiots!"—along with even a few choice words not appropriate to repeat here. Paul had so clearly laid the path for them, yet it was almost as if someone had put a spell on them.

What was the purpose of the Law? Was it intended to justify someone? Did it restrain sin or expose sin?

The Law does not free us; only Christ does that. When God sent His Son to die for us, that sacrifice took away the need to follow all the steps to get to Him and obey some extensive set of rules (yes, that can be tough for us rule followers to get on board with). God's promise here is solid. It's secure. We don't have to turn back to our old ways when the new and free is in front of us. Now we have a way to

Him through confession, faith, and worship. Christ truly does cover all.

Sometimes it can be difficult for us to relate to biblical law. What are some examples of the "law" in your life that is holding you back from true freedom in Christ?

PRAYER FOR FREEDOM

Ask Jesus to help you open your eyes and see yourself as free from any shame or anxiety weighing on you due to a feeling of being imprisoned or confined by your personal "law."

Day Three
FREE SLAVES
Galatians 4:8–31; Romans 6:15–23

We all want freedom. From a child seeking independence from parents to slaves desperate to break free from their masters. Hollywood certainly understands this human longing. Directors and writers know how to tug at our heartstrings through images of what freedom means to those in bondage. We heard the Genie character from *Aladdin* make his own wish for freedom. "But oh, to be free. Not to have to go 'Poof! Whaddaya need?' … To be my own master. Such a thing would be greater than all the magic and all the treasures in all the world."[2] And then Erik "Killmonger" Stevens delivered one of the infamous lines of the movie *Black Panther*: "Bury me in the ocean with my ancestors who jumped from the ships because they knew death was better than bondage."[3]

No one wants to be trapped in bonds of slavery to any man (or even a lamp). Freedom is sought after by everyone who considers themselves to be oppressed. But freedom in Christ is not the same thing as freedom from man. Just think about it—some of the most harshly oppressed people in the world have complete freedom in Christ!

Here comes the tricky part—Paul tells us that, technically, no one is free. It almost feels like a contradiction when we look to Romans 6 and read his words saying that we are all slaves. Isn't that what we are told to escape from? Isn't all slavery bad? Let's take a look.

✒ **Go to the Word:** *Read Romans 6:15–23.*

What did Paul say you used to be?

What are you slaves to now?

In the New Testament, the word *doulos* was used as the word for "servant" or "slave," meaning "someone who belongs to another" or "a bond-slave without any ownership rights of their own."[4] Most modern translations have translated the word to "servant" or "bondservant," likely to soften the word. However, a servant is usually someone who works for their wages and is owed something from their master. But for us as Christ followers, we have nothing to give in return for the payment Jesus offered on the cross for us. We are purchased by the blood of Jesus and are His possessions. We belong to Him; therefore, *doulos*, or *slave*, is the proper word to describe our relationship to Him! The silver lining is, we are far from being oppressed like other slaves we've heard of.

～ **Go to the Word:** *Read through these scriptures and make note of what is offered to us.*

John 8:32

John 8:36

Romans 8:2

✐ *Go to the Word:* *Read Galatians 4:8–31.*

So, here's the real question. We can choose slavery to sin or slavery to Christ (actually, freedom!), but we still find ourselves caught up in bondage. *Why?* Why do we do it when we know the beauty of this relationship offered to us? I can't help but wonder what pushed the Galatians off course. They knew what it was like to be enslaved to their sin, but they got distracted and returned to their old ways once again. The Galatians (and we too) have to realize that the bondage of sin can't hold us back once Christ has set us free. We are able to stand firm; we don't have to submit to our old mind-set of slavery (Galatians 5:1). As slaves to God, we are so free. And we aren't alone in this—we have so many gifts to help us (but more on that later).

Go to Romans 6:4 and complete this paraphrase:

We were _____ along with Jesus into a kind of baptism into death, and just as Christ was _____ from the dead by His Father's glory, so we too may _____.

Look back at Galatians 4:8–11. Paul describes the Galatians as being enslaved by elements and seasons. What kinds of rituals, behaviors, or other things are the "gods" that enslave you at times?

Do you find that you take advantage of your relationship with God? Have you ever run in your self-proclaimed freedom and left Christ out of the picture? How does the idea that we are slaves to God change your view of your relationship with Him?

PRAYER FOR FREEDOM

This idea of being slaves of Christ can seem foreign or uncomfortable to us. Ask God to help you discern what in your will is troubled by this concept and to reveal the ways in which you may have been enslaving yourself to other things besides God.

Day Four
WALKING IN THE SPIRIT
Galatians 5:16–26

I have a lot of girls, and their closets are FULL of clothes. Piles upon piles of adorable outfits that I handpicked for their birthdays or off the sale rack at Target (can I get an "Amen"?). I'm always excited to put together cute little outfits for them and hope they will put everything I've given them to good use.

Yet, every time they go to pick out something to wear, they revert back to the same few tried-and-true pieces: the worn-out T-shirt from that Christmas musical a few years ago, the leggings with a hole in the knee, that dress that I swear I put in the Goodwill stack at least three times. (I mean, where did that even come from?)

This is the thought that goes through my head each time I see them wearing these old things: *Child, why don't you take advantage of the good gifts I've given you? I handpicked those for you. (And they look good on you.)*

And then God clears His throat: "Ahem. Are you hearing yourself, My child? Consider the gifts I've given you that you just let sit and go unused."

Yes, God, I hear You.

Think about it. God has equipped us with so many wonderful things—a closet full of gifts at our disposal—and we so often revert to the old worn-out, tried-and-not-so-true attributes we feel more comfortable in. Let's take some time today to focus on the gifts that God has given us through His Spirit. We'll look at what Paul had to say to the Galatians about the importance of having the Spirit after being released from the Law.

Go to the Word: *Read Galatians 5:16–26.*

Many people would say that Galatians 5:16 is one of the most crucial scriptures on Christian living in the Bible, and I would have to agree. But to many of us, the Holy Spirit is a mystery. Jesus, we know. God the Father, we know. But the Holy Spirit? That's a little trickier.

Francis Chan said it so well in his book *Forgotten God*:

> There is a big gap between what we read in Scripture about the Holy Spirit and how most believers and churches operate today....
>
> I believe that this missing *something* is actually a missing *Someone*—namely, the Holy Spirit. Without Him, people operate in their own strength and only accomplish human-size results. The world is not moved by love or actions that are of human creation.[5]

Thanks for the swift kick in the knees, Mr. Chan. I couldn't agree more, though—how many times do we find ourselves trying to do it all on our own, operating out of our own strength, picking out our worn-out clothes, when we have the Spirit inside us, armed and ready with so much more? I'll be the first in line with my hand raised the highest to say I'm guilty of this.

Write out Galatians 5:16 in your own words.

Look up this scripture in different Bible translations to get a greater scope of meaning. Write down what you learned.

Walking in the Spirit isn't something that is reserved for "special" Christian leaders or certain people. God's Word is for you too, right in the trenches of motherhood—the Holy Spirit is for you too. It's one size fits all. The same Spirit that lives in prominent, successful, bestselling Christian leaders lives in you too.

Paul goes on to tell us in Galatians 5:18 that if we are led by the Spirit, we are not under the Law (again reminding those foolish Galatians—us too!—of whom they should follow). We have a desire for more of God and His goodness that we can choose over the desires of our flesh.

Now, let's take another look at what the Spirit gives us. Maybe you learned these verses as a child in Sunday school, but they are just as important for us to know today as grown-ups. Paul reminds us that we all need the truth of the gospel, even if we think we know it already—so, let's refresh and immerse ourselves in God's Word.

Go to the Word: Read Galatians 5:22-26. List the fruit of the Spirit:

What fruit do you find emerging in your life, and which ones do you never see or put into practice? Why?

When we find ourselves walking in the Spirit, we will live our lives out of loving-kindness, gentleness, and self-control. When we trust Christ to guide our choices and decisions, we will see that we are practicing peace, joy, and patience. You see—those gifts are already in your closet, ready to take and put on. So instead of going to your closet and choosing the worn-out attire of exhaustion, frustration, and bitterness—you can put on kindness, goodness, and faithfulness, and walk on in the Spirit.

PRAYER FOR FREEDOM

Think of one fruit of the Spirit you want to cultivate this week. Write it down here, then ask God to help you work on that quality every day.

WEEK ONE
Group Discussion

STARTER

What did *freedom* look like to you as a child? If you want, bring in a picture or a symbol from your childhood that represents what you saw as freedom and share it with the group.

REVIEW

1. Let's cover some basics:

Who wrote the book of Galatians?

Why is Galatians important?

What is the overall message of this letter?

2. Why did Paul need to remind these Christ followers about the gospel? Do you think today's Christians need to be reminded about the gospel? Give your reasons.

3. Perform a role play. Pretend that the person next to you is not a believer and has just said, "I thought you Christians were supposed to be living according to the

Ten Commandments, but you just seem to pick and choose what laws you want to follow." In your reply, describe what the purpose of the Law was and how Jesus' life, death, and resurrection changed the way Christians viewed the Law.

4. In order to obtain the freedom in Christ we all desire, we have to be enslaved to God. Discuss what this means. How do we sometimes get caught in the bondage of sin?

5. Discuss what it means to "walk in the Spirit" and how that can change your life, your outlook on your freedom in Christ, and your ability to use the gift of the Spirit.

PRAYER FOR FREEDOM

Begin a simple prayer together by asking the Holy Spirit to help each group member grow and increase the practice of one specific fruit of the Spirit. Allow time for each member to speak that one fruit out loud—one that is meaningful to her. Then close the prayer time by asking God to help each one of you to walk more freely in the Spirit.

Room to Reflect

FREEDOM FROM FEAR

What if someone snatches one of my children in the grocery store parking lot? What if the baby burns herself on the stove? What if vaccinations hurt my child? What if not getting the shots is dangerous? What if my child falls behind in school? Did I tell my child I love them enough?

What if, what if, what if!

I don't know about you, but these are all fears I have had. As mothers, we carry the burden of fear with us most of the time. In both the big, life-altering things and the small, seemingly inconsequential things, we are tempted to fear. It is a load we often carry alone, and it takes intentional surrender on our part to walk in freedom instead.

In addition to bearing this weight, we can let fear keep us from achieving the good that the Father has tasked us to accomplish. Fear can paralyze us to the point of uselessness to the Master.

Fear isn't always a life-or-death matter. Fear of what others might say about us or do behind our backs can also keep us from reaching out to others. Fear isolates—it turns our attention to ourselves and takes our focus off the Master and the work He has for us as moms, wives, daughters, friends, and neighbors.

What does the Bible say about fear? How do we choose freedom and reject fear when we are tired and stretched thin?

Day One

THE BONDAGE OF FEAR

Romans 8:15; Psalm 33:8-9; Psalm 23

I could hear Hannah cry out from her bedroom. It was the kind of cry that every mother recognizes—the kind that sends us running when we hear it. You know the one I mean. My girl was hurt and scared. It was our first night home with Emma, our second kiddo, and Hannah had somehow twisted her little wrist in a torn piece of her blanket. The fabric was twisted so tightly, her hand was dark purple. Although this may not sound very dramatic, it felt like life and death for about ten seconds as we quickly cut the fabric from around her wrist.

Fear is deceptive. It makes us feel frantic, irrational, and often hopeless. Thankfully, though, we have been given hope and a good Father we can trust. We can run into His arms and know we will find only truth and love.

Go to the Word: Romans 8:15. Write out the verse in the space below.

To whom is Paul speaking? (Look back at Romans 8:12-14.)

Some translations say that we have received a "Spirit of adoption." What do you think that means?

According to Romans 8:15, we are chosen and beloved children of God. We are not slaves, forced to remain. We are bought with a price, valued, and loved. As we approach the Lord in prayer in light of this verse, our relationship with the Father becomes the basis for expelling fear and being bold when approaching His throne (Hebrews 4:16).

At this point, you might be wondering, *Wait, doesn't it say in the Bible that we are supposed to FEAR the Lord?*

Did you know, fear can actually be a form of worship? Proverbs tells us that the fear of the Lord is the beginning of wisdom (Proverbs 1:7; 2:5; 9:10).

How do you think fear can be a form of worship?

This kind of fear is not polite respectfulness before Yahweh God; this is holy terror in consideration of His raw power. The Lord is potency personified. His decisions have finality; His words carry weight. When Scripture states, "Thus saith the Lord," a wise person will listen and obey. God's Word is powerful. With a few simple words, the universe came from nothing. A healthy fear of the Lord recognizes the gravity of who the Lord is. He is not someone to be trifled with or taken lightly.

*➢ **Go to the Word:** Read Psalm 33:8-9:*

> Let the whole earth fear the LORD;
> let all the inhabitants of the world stand
> in awe of him.
> For he spoke, and it came into being;
> he commanded, and it came into
> existence.

In the verses above, circle who should fear the Lord. Then underline what He has done.

So, we are left with two different big ideas. We are not to be slaves to fear, but we are to fear God. How do these thoughts even go together? We read the answer in one of the most popular passages of the Bible.

*➢ **Go to the Word:** Read Psalm 23.*

This is such a comforting psalm for so many people. It highlights the love and care that our God has for us. The context of this song of praise shows how God treats those who are

His—those who claim Him as their shepherd. That's important to remember for the verses we will concentrate on.

List a few ways we see the Lord care for us in Psalm 23.

Look at verse 4. This verse talks about some pretty intense situations. Walking through the valley of death does not sound pleasant, but the sheep that trusts the shepherd is totally free from fear. If the sheep were in bondage to fear, he would not walk through the valley of death.

In that same verse, it says the rod and staff bring comfort to the sheep. This makes complete sense when we think of those implements as tools to defend the sheep from outside threats, such as wolves. These shepherding tools are a display of the physical power and violence the shepherd is capable of, but the staff is also used to guide the sheep back to the flock. The sheep depends on the power and wisdom of the shepherd, and when it feels the staff applied, it complies. Fear in the proper context of a relationship with Creator God makes all the difference.

PRAYER FOR FREEDOM

As you approach the Lord in prayer, remember that your relationship with the Father and your knowledge of Him are what allow you to come to Him boldly.

Day Two
FEAR NOT
Isaiah 41:10; Hebrews 13:6

I remember as a young girl being terrified of Morticia, the mom from *The Addams Family*. A friend had gifted us an *Addams Family* board game, and that silly game haunted my dreams, I kid you not! I would have nightmares about her creepy black nails and her long black hair. Obviously, Morticia is a fictional character and in no way a threat, but in the dark of night, in my mind, I worked myself up to believe that she was truly something to be fearful of.

As children, we find many things fear inducing. In most cases, though, when the parents we trust tell us "You don't need to be afraid," we trust them and our fear can subside.

Go to the Word: Read Isaiah 41:10, then write down how you feel when you read this verse.

In Isaiah 41:10, our Father, whom we can trust, is telling us, "You need not be afraid. I am bigger than all of this. I will hold you."

Fear is often thought of as an emotion. However, it is not something that simply happens to a person. Fear is something we can control. We can allow it to exist, and we can feed it. It can grow and conquer us if left alone to multiply. Fear can lead to despair, to feelings of utter hopelessness—a terrible attitude to fall into. However, for someone in the darkness of this world without Jesus, fear and despair are a logical conclusion. Without Jesus, where can we find hope?

In what ways do these verses make you feel hopeful?
   Isaiah 40:31

Psalm 33:20–22

   Let's shed some more light on the context of Isaiah 41. Isaiah was a prophet for a long time in Judah, and he served the Lord during a trying time. The enemies of Israel in the north were also moving in on Judah in the south. There were, however, good things happening during Isaiah's ministry, as well as terrifying things. Isaiah 41:10 is part of the Lord's encouragement of the kingdom of Judah. He tells them twice in this one verse not to fear.

Read the verses below and note how the Lord showed Himself to Judah. These acts of faithfulness helped the people to trust that when the Lord told them they need not fear, they could trust Him.
   2 Chronicles 20:20–22

Hosea 1:7

Isaiah 45:2–3

   The Lord wants us to know and trust Him. Part of the way we do that is by constantly asking Him to reveal Himself to us and by recounting the things He has already done. Just like small children, we struggle to trust a stranger. The Lord need not be a stranger to us. He has given us His Word and the Holy Spirit to speak to us and reveal His character. Before we can fully trust Him, we must fully know Him.

Go to the Word: *Read Hebrews 13:5-6 and note what effect the Lord revealing Himself has:*

How has the Lord showed you in the past that He is on your side?

PRAYER FOR FREEDOM

Take a few moments to share with the Lord some things in your life that are tempting you to fear.

I feel fearful when

I desire freedom from

I need not fear because

Day Three
THE ANTI-FEAR FORMULA
2 Timothy 1:7

I grew up with a dad who could fix or build just about any-thing. If my doll lost an arm, Dad would fix it. If my cassette tape came unraveled, Dad would fix it. If we wanted a play-house, Dad would build it. I remember working alongside him, watching him use different tools for different tasks and learning what each contraption was intended for. Dad had tools for everything, and his collection was ever growing; it still is today. Just like Dad and his tools, we need to be equipped appropriately to combat fear in our lives. You can't drive a nail without a hammer, and you can't combat fear without Christ. We have talked this week about how fear binds us, and God commands us to fear not. Today we are learning about the tools we have been given to help dis-mantle fear.

Go to the Word: 2 Timothy 1:7.

God has not given us a "spirit of fear." What has He given us instead?

When Paul wrote this letter to Timothy, he had a couple of different reasons for writing. First, this is most likely one of the last letters Paul wrote before his death. This is his farewell letter to his close friend and protégé.

If you knew you would not be alive much longer, what words would you write to those close to you?

Second, Paul wrote to encourage Timothy in the ministry. Timothy was young but capable. He was perhaps not always taken as seriously as Paul or one of the other older apostles, even though Paul was in the habit of sending Timothy to speak and deliver messages on his behalf.

Paul wanted to encourage Timothy to hold fast and continue the course. Paul talked about them having received a Spirit of power, love, and sound judgment, or self-control.

How is power opposed to fear? Fear takes power away from the person who is afraid. This person gives respect and authority to the one they fear. Ever seen a cartoon where an elephant is afraid of a mouse? This joke is funny because it is ridiculous. Elephants are massive compared to mice. Mice have no venom or anything that would give an elephant pause. But still, fear causes the elephant to forget his power. When an individual recognizes his power, fear is diminished.

Based on the verses listed below, give a definition of *power*:
    Luke 21:25-28

Acts 1:8; 2:22–24

Ephesians 1:20–23

How is love opposed to fear? Love is a selfless expression; it's focused on others. When fear is present, feelings tend to turn inward. Fear causes people to abandon others, while love motivates them to defend and protect in the face of opposition. Love becomes the basis for many forms of courage. Fathers run into burning buildings and mothers lift buses off their children because of love.

Based on the verses listed below, give a definition of *love*:
   Matthew 6:24

   Matthew 22:37

   Romans 5:8

How is sound judgment opposed to fear? Sound judgment is linked closely with self-control. It allows someone to assess a situation for what it is and not be overcome with fear. Being self-controlled allows one to act in integrity and faithfulness rather than reacting in fear.

Based on the verses listed below, give a definition of *sound judgment*:

Mark 5:14

Titus 2:6–8

1 Peter 4:7

Which one of these three (power, love, sound judgment) do you need more of in your life?

PRAYER FOR FREEDOM

Write a prayer to the Lord asking for a spirit of power, love, or sound judgment.

Day Four
PEACE
Philippians 4:7; John 14:27; Matthew 26:36-56

My idea of peace is a quiet house, a warm bath, or a mug of coffee. After a hectic day, my husband will often come home and recognize that I am teetering on the edge of insanity, and he graciously takes our darling children far away for an hour or two. I can tidy up, cook dinner in peace, or really do whatever my weary heart desires. This is a precious gift my husband gives to me, and as glorious as that gift is, it can't even come close to comparing with the peace the Lord provides.

Go to the Word: *Read Philippians 4:7: "And the peace of God, which surpasses all understanding, will guard your hearts and minds in Christ Jesus."*

Underline the phrase in Philippians 4:7 that describes the peace of God.

We literally cannot fathom the peace we have in Christ! It is so much greater than our human minds can grasp! Often, *peace* is perceived as a passive word, but in this context, *peace* is active! It is active in our hearts and our minds! The peace of God GUARDS our hearts and minds. We are being protected and cared for by the God of the universe.

What do you think we are being guarded from?

✎ **Go to the Word:** *Read John 14:27: "Peace I leave with you. My peace I give to you. I do not give to you as the world gives. Don't let your heart be troubled or fearful."*

Write out this part of the verse three times: "Peace I leave with you. My peace I give to you."

This passage is even more powerful when you consider that these words of Jesus preceded some amazingly huge failures by the disciples and some of their most frightening days—days when they would desperately long for peace. After Jesus gave this and many other encouraging words, they went out to the garden of Gethsemane.

✎ **Go to the Word:** *Read Matthew 26:36–56. Summarize what happens in these verses.*

Jesus was starting to feel the weight of the sin of humanity and what it would cost. Just as the first sin was accomplished in a garden, the answer to that sin would also be found in one.

Peter, James, and John could not even stay awake to pray while Jesus knelt in emotional and spiritual agony, until the crowd of clamoring men arrived.

Jesus knew it was time to be led to His shame and death. He knew that He would endure terrible pain. However, it was not Jesus who ran in fear. His disciples ran when Jesus made it clear that He would not be fighting the accusers that evening. Jesus, even in the face and in the midst of intense suffering, was the picture of peace. He did not raise His voice; He did not use His famous sarcasm and wit. No, Jesus peacefully walked with His traitorous companion to a court full of lies and disdain.

What do you think the disciples feared that caused them to run away?

What are some things that might be causing you to fear and run away in this season of life?

Outside the courtroom drama, Peter lied to those around him when questioned concerning his relationship to Jesus. Peter had no peace in his heart and ran weeping from the scene.

The kind of peace that Jesus had did not come because of His circumstances. He was not with friends or supported by allies. He was not treated kindly or justly. The only one who showed a measure of compassion to Jesus was Pontius Pilate, who told the crowds that he found no fault in this man. But there was no pacifying the violent crowd. A mob wanted to torture and kill Jesus in the most brutal way possible, and Jesus, the Lamb of God, was silent before His shearers (Isaiah 53:7). Even when on the cross, His concern was for His accusers—He asked the Father to forgive them because of the ignorance of their actions.

Can you imagine being filled with such immense love and peace that, as you die, you would pray for those who hate you and want to see you dead?

Jesus was not peaceful because He experienced peace in this world or from this world. He had peace because He knew the outcome of the story. He knew that there was rest beyond this world, beyond the work of suffering. He knew that there was a throne at the end of the road, and He knew the promises that the Father had made were faithful and true. There would be an end to suffering; sin and death would be conquered. He had peace because He placed His faith in the words of His Father and saw the race as being worth running (Hebrews 12:1–3).

Peace is not something you experience; it is a virtue you bring to your circumstance. Are your children tearing apart your house? You can have peace, because they will eventually nap (or collapse from exhaustion). Did you receive your diagnosis from the oncologist? You can have peace, because you know that Jesus knows suffering and will bring encouragement. Did you lose your house? You can have peace, because the Lord has promised to care for your needs.

Fear and worry are the dispellers of peace. Fear and anxiety come from meditating on the potential evil outcomes of a situation—how bad things can get. Well, if you play that game, fear will be hard to beat, and peace will be hard to find. Instead, what has the Lord already said? (Go back up and read John 14:27.)

What does Jesus promise to leave with us?

The world hands out fear like samples at Costco; always another batch in the toaster oven, and we clamor for it. Jesus offers a feast of peace instead. Our solutions for fear are often temporary, ineffectual, and weak when compared to the enduring, powerful, and over-the-top amazing promises of God. The results Jesus offers require patience, endurance, and humility. Wait patiently on the Lord!

Speak some truth into your life and heart today. Kick fear to the curb; it's not welcome here!

PRAYER FOR FREEDOM

What is one thing you are waiting on and seeking the Lord about? Pray about that today.

WEEK TWO
Group Discussion

STARTER

Talk about a fear you had as a child. What was that about? Has it stayed with you into adulthood?

REVIEW

1. How does fear play a part in your life? Where does it show up the most?

2. Do you think you are currently operating out of a spirit of fear or out of a Spirit of adoption? Why?

3. Share a testimony of the Lord's faithfulness in your life.

4. How does knowing the Lord help us combat fear in our lives?

5. How can you bring peace to your life today (regardless of your circumstances)?

PRAYER FOR FREEDOM

Let each person choose a person to pray for in the group. Allow time for people to listen to each other's fears, concerns, and needs, and then have time for silent prayer. Close the prayer by praying a blessing of peace on the group (you could use Jesus' words from John 14:27).

Room to Reflect

FREEDOM FROM EXPECTATION

There are so many expectations placed on us as women and as moms. Sometimes it feels like an endless cycle and a monster of responsibilities that will eat us alive. Pay the bills, prepare dinner, sign the school folders, do the laundry, clean the house, keep up with friends, maintain a good marriage, keep the kids alive.

It's just a bit much.

But let's be honest—most of these expectations are things we put on ourselves. We are trying to measure up, do the best, and keep all the plates spinning. My husband always laughs at me when I apologize for the overflowing laundry basket and reminds me he's perfectly capable of washing his own underwear.

We have these expectations for who we should be, but are those from the Lord? *Nope.* God is not an evil dictator expecting us to do a list of things to measure up or be good enough—that's the beauty we find in freedom in Christ. As we learned in week one, we are free from the Law, and we no longer have to obey a list of detailed guidelines to follow Him. We simply choose to follow Him, and we find freedom there.

This week, we are going to learn from the greatest Teacher, Jesus, and see how His interactions with some people can show us a thing or two about what God truly expects from us. Be ready to walk into this week and find some freedom from expectations. Go ahead and still put in that load of laundry, though (if that's on your list for today), because we aren't talking about walking away from your responsibilities—just claiming a little freedom along the way.

Day One
DISCOVERING TRUE WORSHIP
John 4:1–42

Let's get real for a minute—many people can turn the gospel into bad, negative news for women. These people might assume that the status of "more important Christ follower" goes to the men and let them do the heavy lifting. And this becomes especially bad news for moms. We are doing the not-so-glamorous, in-the-trenches work that is unseen and sometimes un-thanked (except on Mother's Day, when doughnuts cover all wounds).

But can I tell you something I love? Jesus spent time with women. And by spending time with them (particularly in the culture of the first century), He showed that women were valuable and important. Not just the women who were leaders, wealthy, or well known, but women just like you and me. The imperfect women, the unseen women, the women doing the hard work in the everyday world. He took time to sit with them and listen to them. Let that be a beautiful reminder: you are valued by the Savior of the world.

Today, we meet up with Jesus in Samaria, taking a break in the course of His travels. He's tired and weary (I find comfort in the fact that Jesus sometimes felt the aches and pains and exhaustion we all feel from life) and makes a stop at the well at noon.

Because indoor plumbing wasn't a thing yet, the well was an important place. Not only was this where everyone came to get water to use for their families—it was also a social gathering place. I imagine it was like the Chick-fil-A play place on a busy Thursday at lunch hour or the local coffee shop on a

Saturday morning, a spot where many women meet to catch up and chat.

However, this story is set in the Middle East, so the hottest point of the day is not the best time for gathering at the well. And yet here we find two strangers meeting—Jesus and a Samaritan woman.

✐ **Go to the Word:** *Read John 4:1–26.*

Write down some characteristics you learn about our woman at the well. What do you notice about what she says and how she speaks to this unknown traveler? What does Jesus point out about her?

Let's talk for a minute about these "five husbands." We have to remember to try to see the text through the cultural perspective of the time. In first-century Palestine, women couldn't just make a Tuesday afternoon of it, stroll to a lawyer's office, file for divorce, and stop by Starbucks for a grande caramel macchiato on the way home. Divorces being requested by women wasn't acceptable in their culture; therefore, her previous husbands must have either divorced her or died. She could have been labeled a lot of things, but she was likely not a reckless divorcer.

Another thing to consider is that Roman marriage laws stipulated that only freeborn people could marry other freeborn people. This excluded the millions of former slaves who lived in the Roman Empire. Again, we don't know her status, but she could have been living as a concubine (someone of a lower class who lives with a man and his wives in a polygamous arrangement). Women weren't considered equals to men and depended on male family members to provide for them and give them shelter. So, it's possible the only way for her to take care of herself was to go from husband to husband.

While we will probably never know exactly what the circumstances of this Samaritan woman's life were, we can still take note of this: Jesus paid no attention to her social status (though His disciples did—see their reaction in John 4:27). He met her there with purpose and on purpose.

Consider the conversation between Jesus and the woman: What does Jesus say is the difference between living water and the water she is drawing from the well?

What is the result of the living water?

How does Jesus respond to her statement about worship?

The Samaritan woman discovers in this encounter with Jesus that true worship is not found in the confines of a building or within a group of people. She also realizes that living water is not found with a man, a marriage, or whatever she might be caught up in.

This does not excuse us from corporate worship, because Jesus also taught the importance of gathering together, but one of the things that created divisions among the Jews and the Samaritans was that they disagreed on the location for proper worship of God. Jesus, in His usual way, is turning these beliefs on their head and saying that they've all got it wrong. Living water doesn't come from a well, but from the Spirit of God. Proper worship doesn't happen on a mountain or in a cathedral or even in a tiny chapel, but in the heart of every person who comes to the Father in Spirit and in truth.

God is bigger than our expectations.

Consider your well. Where has Jesus met you in your weakness and changed you, offering you living water?

Are you settling for a lukewarm drink at midday to avoid being seen? Are you willing to meet Jesus there at your well, in your brokenness, and accept the living water that He has to offer? He does not expect you to have it all together. He did not wait for the Samaritan woman to go and prove herself before He offered her freedom from thirst; He met her right in the midst of her weakness and brokenness and offered her eternal life. He'll do the same for you.

PRAYER FOR FREEDOM

Ask Christ to meet you at your well today. Tell Him the truth about your situation, and ask Him to give you living water.

Day Two
THIS DOES NOT DEFINE YOU
Luke 8:1–3; John 20:1–18

I have this particular low point in my history that I'm not proud of. I hit rock bottom after having three kids in under three years, and it wasn't pretty. In that season, I was sure God was done using me. I couldn't see through that pain how He could possibly do anything with me again, and I expected that to be the end of any kind of ministry for me. I was okay with that; I figured I was damaged goods and I'd done my best up until that point.

God had other plans—and I should have known better. When I was able to share the depths and hard parts of my story in my book, I couldn't believe the feedback I got from women who had walked through or were walking through the same things. My friend Brittany texted me the week my book released and said, "Remember that time of struggle with post-partum depression and anxiety? See what the Lord has done with that all of these years later!?"

She was right. God did that. Not me in my own strength, or else it would have been a massive crash-and-burn failure. But only God can take our complete weakness and broken-ness and turn it into something amazing He can use for His glory. I'm reminded of this through the story of one of my Bible heroes—Mary Magdalene.

Mary Magdalene was a dear friend and faithful follower of Jesus. She was the most prominent woman who accompa-nied Him from Galilee to Jerusalem and was mentioned in the Gospels fourteen times (which is very uncommon, because most women in the Bible aren't even named!). This hints at the significance of her life and her role in Jesus' inner circle. But this isn't where her story began.

~~~ ***Go to the Word:*** *Read Luke 8:1-3.*

What do you learn about Mary Magdalene from these verses?

What was her rock bottom that she struggled with before she followed Jesus?

Based on this glimpse of her past, what do you think the expectation would have been of her?

Mary met Jesus and found freedom. We learn about this group of women who traveled with Jesus that all had been healed of evil spirits or illness. Mary Magdalene had seven demons cast out of her. We also read that they all came from wealth, because they were able to provide for Jesus and His disciples on their journeys by "supporting them from their possessions" (one was the wife of one of the king's officials). Mary Magdalene walked and talked with Jesus, doing real life with Him and His disciples. We're not told the specifics of her demons or what she had walked through in her past, but we do know that no one is too broken for Jesus to use. Our demons don't define us.

Go to the Word: *Read John 20:1–18.*

The report of Jesus' death and burial is incredibly significant in Mary Magdalene's story. When Jesus was abandoned by His followers, Mary Magdalene stayed by Him as He was dying on the cross. She saw Him buried—and then came back to find the empty tomb on the third day. She is considered to be the primary witness to history's greatest event. (Can you imagine?!)

In the gospel of John, we get the most detailed version: Mary finds the empty tomb and runs to tell Peter and another disciple, who then comes back with her to see that the tomb is indeed empty. The men leave, but Mary Magdalene remains at the tomb, weeping for her Lord.

As she is crying, angels appear in the tomb, and she talks with them. Then, turning around, she mistakes Jesus for a gardener at the entrance and wonders if He has taken the body of her Lord away.

But Jesus only has to call her by name for Mary to recognize Him and address Him as *Rabboni*, meaning "teacher." When she hears her name in His voice, her eyes are opened, and she knows her Lord. Her response is like that of the sheep described by Jesus in John 10:3–4, following their shepherd:

"He calls his own sheep by name and leads them out.... The sheep follow him because they know his voice."

In what ways are you so distracted by your own situations, grief, and pain that you sometimes fail to recognize when Jesus is calling your name?

Jesus is the Good Shepherd, calling us by name, reminding us we are called by Him to follow Him and do His work. This beautiful encounter with Mary Magdalene shows us how Jesus is a personal friend, and even though He has a great mission, He takes the time to call us each by name. He does not define us by our past, our missteps, or our struggles. He frees us and uses us right where we are.

Mary's life took her from the demonic to the discipled. After having evil spirits cast out of her, she was freed to become one of the most prominent witnesses of Jesus' earthly ministry, death, and resurrection.

What are some changes that need to happen in your life to get rid of sin and help you walk in freedom?

PRAYER FOR FREEDOM

Imagine for your prayer time today that you are in Mary's san-
dals, meeting Jesus for the first time after His resurrection.
What would you say to Him?

Day Three
HOW WILL THIS CHANGE YOU?
Luke 19:1–10

"Mama, which one's the bad guy?" my son asks, every time we turn on a TV show or play with his action figures. I point out Thanos in his Avengers set and tell him, "That's the bad guy!" Even at the age of three, he knows the difference between good and bad, as he runs off to have good fight evil.

We spent the last couple of days looking at the way Jesus interacted with and treated women who likely had reputations for themselves, and negative expectations placed on them by their communities. We saw how Jesus honored and respected them. He didn't look down on them or disregard them because of their past or their sin.

Today, we're going to learn about one of the least favorite people of the time, who happens to be a man: the tax collector. If first-century three-year-olds had had action figures, their "bad guys" might have been tax collectors. So, what exactly was a tax collector, and why were they disliked so much?

There are a few reasons why tax collectors were viewed so badly. No one likes to have to pay the government, and this was the case just as much then as it is now! The Roman Empire was oppressive to people, and the collection of taxes wasn't exactly fair. But to make matters worse, most tax collectors in the Bible were actually Jews working for this much-despised government. And it was common knowledge that tax collectors cheated the people they collected from—they charged more than they were required and filled their own pockets with the excess. People were resigned to the fact that this was how the system worked. It wasn't right, but it happened, and hence, the hatred toward tax collectors grew.

Pretend you are a first-century mom. What expectations might you have about a person known to be a tax collector? Would you want to hang out with that person? Would you want your kids to know him?

So, now you can see why the Pharisees were so shocked (and annoyed) whenever Jesus was eating a meal "with sinners and tax collectors" (Mark 2:15-16). The Pharisees were all about following the rules, and any Jew who didn't follow the rules was just horribly wrong in their book. While most people considered tax collectors as the lowest of the low and the enemy, Jesus saw them as something more. Let's take a look at His interaction with one specific tax collector and how it changed the man.

*✐ **Go to the Word:** Read Luke 19:1-10.*

Immediately, what facts do you learn about Zacchaeus?

What was shocking in this story about Jesus' response to Zacchaeus? If you had been in Jesus' position, what would you have done?

Did you notice something in the description about Zacchaeus? He was labeled the "chief tax collector." I don't think this story was placed here by accident, or that this was some random meeting at the sycamore tree. God knew what He was doing in this moment. Zacchaeus, being the chief tax collector, would have likely been well known—and well hated.

You see, Zacchaeus messed up. Big time. Jericho was one of the wealthiest cities in Palestine, in a very fertile area of Judea. It was a bustling trade city and housed many of the wealthiest families. All that to say—taxes in this city would have been expensive.[1] Zacchaeus's job would have already made him filthy rich, even without cheating people on their taxes. But still, he did it. This guy was just the worst. A true bad guy.

Zacchaeus climbed to the top of a tree to catch a glimpse of this Jesus guy. If you went to Sunday school as a child, you know that Zacchaeus was a wee little man (and a wee little man was he). Likely under five feet tall, he had to get up high to see Jesus over the heads of the crowd.

Now, no matter who you were, it wasn't common to invite yourself into someone's home. And I doubt it was all that common to send invitations up a tree. And for Jesus the Messiah—the man everyone had come out to see—to even speak to and much less invite Himself to stay with short, stingy, thieving Zacchaeus, the lowest of the low, would have turned some heads for sure.

What was Zacchaeus's immediate response to the invitation Jesus offered?

How was Zacchaeus changed this day? What can change in you because of the freedom Jesus offers?

What is freedom? Freedom is when we find ourselves at the top of a tree as the lowest of the low, completely lost, craning our neck for a glimpse of Jesus because He might just be able to save us from ourselves (whether we know we want Him to or not!). Freedom is allowing the grace and gift of Jesus to change us completely. Freedom is dropping everything, jumping down out of that tree, and saying yes to follow Him. Freedom is not even minding what it costs us to make things right, because we're so overjoyed to be seen and known and loved by Jesus. Freedom is breaking through society's expectations to accept Jesus' salvation.

PRAYER FOR FREEDOM

If you haven't accepted Jesus' invitation to follow Him and receive salvation, think about doing that today. If you have received His salvation, but still feel low, ask Jesus to help you see yourself just as He sees you—loved by Him.

Day Four

SHATTERING EXPECTATIONS

Matthew 4; Mark 1; Luke 5-6, 19; John 5, 8

I grew up in the "Bible Belt." I was raised in the church, and I knew my Bible inside and out by the time I went off to college. While I'm very grateful for my roots and all I learned about Scripture, there is something I missed. This was no one's fault but my own, because I just didn't get it. I didn't grasp who Jesus was until I was an adult and began to really study the Bible for myself. I had put Jesus and His Word into a little box, and I thought it was meek and traditional. And I thought there was something wrong with me because I didn't feel meek or traditional.

I eventually learned that Jesus was anything but traditional. And I found so much freedom in that, that I hope you have met that Jesus too. Today, we are going to look a bit at the life of Jesus—how He shattered all expectations and what we can learn from that.

List some character traits you feel Jesus has.

When we think about Jesus being the *Son of God*, we probably imagine He hung out at the synagogue a lot, right? Plenty of time behind the pulpit, teaching and ministering to the people who came in the building. Makes sense, right?

My husband is a pastor and my kids joke sometimes that the church is home, because we spend a lot of time there. But there's a depth of painful truth in that.

This is something my husband and I discuss often as being a part of church leadership—if we are only seen inside the walls of the church, are we really able to reach the people of our community? Are we really able to reach people where they are and show them Jesus if we are behind the walls of—let's be honest—a sometimes pretty intimidating building?

Let's take a look at where Jesus met with people.

Go to the Word: *Read the following scriptures and make a note of where Jesus met with and called people to follow Him. What stands out to you about these instances?*

Matthew 4:21-22

Mark 1:29-31

Luke 19:1-10

John 5:1-15

Many would have expected that the Messiah would come and always preach in the synagogues and follow all the rules, but no. Jesus broke the mold from the beginning. He showed us there is freedom from the expectations of what people think we are supposed to do to follow Him and lead others to follow Him.

Jesus asked questions. He connected with feelings and emotions. He knew that people needed a minute to think on things themselves before responding or acting. He left space for questions, conversations, and interruptions. Let's look at a few more examples of His reactions to people and make note of the questions Jesus asked, how He interacted, and how that might differ from what would be expected of THE Messiah.

Luke 5:17–26

Luke 6:6–11

John 8:1–11

As we learned through the interaction with Zacchaeus, Jesus could often be found in the company of the worst of the worst, the lowest of the low. He didn't hide behind a pulpit and preach a message; He went out and lived it for all to see and understand. He knew how to take initiative and how to meet people where they would be, on their turf. He didn't wait for people to come to Him.

We've frequently heard Jesus referred to as a "friend to sinners," not because He ignored sin (He hated sin!), but because Jesus was the one to offer freedom to those who wanted it. We are all sinners, and Jesus meets with us right where we are in the midst of our sin and messes to give us freedom!

Now that we've dug a little deeper into who Jesus was, make another character trait list based on what you read

about Him today. What qualities does Jesus have? How would you like to be like Him?

PRAYER FOR FREEDOM

Look over your list of Jesus' character traits. Circle one that you'd like to be known for in your life, and ask God to help you shatter expectations in the way you take after your Lord.

WEEK THREE
Group Discussion

STARTER

Think about someone you know, or a celebrity who really shattered your expectations about him or her, and share how that impacted you (in either a good or bad way).

REVIEW

1. Talk about how the interactions with Jesus affected the lives of the people we read about this week.

The woman at the well met Jesus and

Mary Magdalene met Jesus and

Zacchaeus met Jesus and

2. Discuss ways that Jesus meets us in our weakness and how that can change us. How does it free us from the expectations the world puts on us?

3. Despite Mary Magdalene's past, Jesus offered her freedom from her demons and found value in her. What does

that tell you about your life, no matter what your past circumstances may be?

4. Zacchaeus was willing to give up his greed, pay back what was stolen, and make major changes after his encounter with Jesus. It's not likely that you have the reputation or track record that Zacchaeus did, but what can we learn from this interaction? What does it teach us about the gospel?

5. We can find a lot of freedom from expectations of who we think we should be by reflecting on the life Jesus lived. Talk about the expectations you think are on yourself and which ones you'd like to be free of so you can find freedom in Christ.

PRAYER FOR FREEDOM

Shatter expectations for prayer time by praying all together, out loud, at the same time for however long each person wants and about whatever you want to pray about.

FREEDOM FROM JUDGMENT

We've all done it. You walk past that girl with the see-through pants and think, *Doesn't she own a mirror?!* You park next to someone with a heavily dented bumper and think, *Wow, someone needs to learn how to drive!* You open Instagram to a heavily edited, staged photo of a friend's living room and think, *Why does she have to be so fake?*

Judgment comes so naturally to us; it is scary. We all judge others and we are all judged by others. We almost can't help ourselves. But judgment can lead to insecurity, discontentment, and even hatred if we aren't careful. It creates barriers to community and prevents us from growing in relationships. Criticism and comparison negatively impact both the accuser and the accused. Even though we are prone to point out the flaws of others, that doesn't mean we are incapable of controlling the impulse.

If only we were free. Well, we can be! We are offered freedom directly from Jesus. When Jesus died, He offered us freedom from the burden of having to respond to accusations. His blood is enough to handle not only our past sins but our future ones as well. So, let's not waste any more time. Let's be free!

Day One

COMPARISON
Proverbs 14:30; Galatians 6:4–5; Ephesians 2:8–9

We live in a culture that has an expectation of awareness, of being noticed. Just take a glance at your favorite social media stream and it's clear that our attention is stretched in an incredible number of directions. We're looking at everyone's meal pics. One post about someone's healthy breakfast, homemade breakfast, or guilty pleasure breakfast, for instance, can make us look at our bowl of cold cereal and cringe in mediocrity. Maybe a flower in a vase will help. Perhaps some fruit will add color. Before we know it, we have taken what could have just been a candid photo of an everyday moment and turned it into a marketing campaign. This kind of reaction to comparison can be kind of funny, and some people think these mini photo shoots can be fun, but there are others who see the crafted "candids" as joy thieves.

When comparison holds hands with a judgmental spirit, it can be used by the enemy to rob us of simple blessings and daily joys. An instant coffee could be shared by friends, but compare your pic to a beautifully staged Le Creuset French press with fancy mugs and artisan coffee beans and suddenly a perfectly good moment of shared happiness is turned into borderline shame. And this is only coffee we're talking about. The list of ways we compare ourselves to one another is endless—and for what?

Ninety-nine percent of the time, it's all a lie. Staged pictures of a beautiful lunch, with the screaming child kept just outside the frame. An artful angle on a beautifully styled living room, with all the clutter shoved into the corner. We are comparing ourselves to an unrealistic standard that doesn't even truly exist.

Comparison of this kind leads to a dangerous type of fear in our lives. A fear of comparison, of falling short, can take a specific blessing and make us feel inadequate, when in reality we have been given exactly what we need for the task we have in front of us. Can you imagine Jesus giving you a gracious blessing and then feeling ashamed by it because it doesn't make for as nice of a picture as someone else's "blessing"? Jesus doesn't give junk gifts, but fear can lead us to this conclusion. What's even more dangerous is that it leads to envy.

Envy is a feeling of seeing someone else's blessing and wanting it to the point of having negative feelings or even downright hatred toward that person for having it. Sometimes we don't even want the thing—we just don't want that other person to have it. Comparison blinds us to what we have already been given. It's as if we are telling our Creator that He didn't do enough for us, that He made a mistake.

Go to the Word: *Read Proverbs 14:30: "A tranquil heart is life to the body, but jealousy is rottenness to the bones."*

This verse uses a vivid example of what comparison can do to someone. The rotting of someone's bones is serious. Our whole body is given structure with our bones. Our skeleton is our body's foundation.

Think of a time when comparison with someone else robbed you of your joy. What happened?

Has there ever been a time when envy has impacted your friendships? What was going on with your attitude at that time?

Let's think of this freedom from comparison in another way.

Go to the Word: *Read Galatians 6:4–5: "Let each person examine his own work, and then he can take pride in himself alone, and not compare himself with someone else. For each person will have to carry his own load."*

How often do you take pride in something you've accomplished without comparing it to what someone else has done? What causes you to want to make comparisons?

What do you think "each person will have to carry his own load" means here?

The Lord wants us to reflect on our own work and be able to boast in our deeds. Perhaps this sounds odd when we read it because of how we have been taught the principle in Ephesians 2:8–9.

What is the context of Ephesians 2:8–9? What is there to boast about (or not)?

We are not supposed to look at our deeds (or anyone else's, other than Jesus') and see them as the basis for our salvation. However, we should be able to evaluate how we live and what we do daily and see the work of the Spirit in making us more like Jesus. We are encouraged to look at our actions and compare them to Jesus, who is our true example, and not compare them with those around us (1 John 2:6).

When we look at others, we are tempted to do as little as possible to edge out someone else in doing good. But when we look at Jesus, we can encourage ourselves to grow in true righteousness, and see holiness as our standard of living (Matthew 5:48).

PRAYER FOR FREEDOM

Ask God to do whatever it takes to free you from the blindness and shame that come along with comparisons. Be honest with yourself and with God about when you are most vulnerable to this kind of problem. After you pray about it, ask a friend to keep you accountable.

Day Two

LEGALISM

Matthew 5:17–48; Galatians 3:10–14

Have you ever known a perfect Goody Two-shoes? You know the kind of person I'm talking about—that one mom who always has the perfect hair, the perfectly clean minivan, and the kids who are perfect mini versions of her. When she greets you, you can't help but feel as though she is looking down on you. I know the impulse is to pass quick judgment on her too, but what does the Lord ask of us? Is He wanting us to try harder to earn His favor? The truth is, often the people who look like they have it all together are the ones in need of grace.

Legalism is "the belief that salvation demands or depends upon total obedience to the letter of the law,"[1] and there are many who hold to this notion, at least in part. During the time of Jesus, the Pharisees were identified as being practitioners of this idea. They wanted everyone to adhere strictly to the laws of the Jews. However, Jesus opposed this idea throughout His entire ministry.

In the gospel of Matthew, Jesus preached to His disciples while on a mountain. Through His words, we see that Jesus' concept of law and righteousness was different from that of the Pharisees, and of the world.

*～ **Go to the Word:** Read Matthew 5:17–20.*

Jesus stated that He did not come to abolish the Law but to fulfill it. Now when Jesus used the term *Law* or *Law and the Prophets*, He was speaking of the entire Old Testament. To say that someone would fulfill the Law would mean that person accomplished the works of the Law perfectly and completely without any violations, but it also implies more than that. If the Law could be fulfilled, that would mean it would cease to be a binding covenant. Jesus then spent the rest of Matthew 5 discussing the Law and the concept of righteousness.

For each of the passages that follow, record the "You have heard that it was said" command that Jesus references and the "But I tell you" statements that Jesus makes.

*➬ **Go to the Word:** Read Matthew 5:21–26.*

You have heard that it was said

But I tell you

*➬ **Go to the Word:** Read Matthew 5:27–30.*

You have heard that it was said

But I tell you

*➬ **Go to the Word:** Read Matthew 5:31–32.*

You have heard that it was said

But I tell you

Go to the Word: Read Matthew 5:33–37.

You have heard that it was said

But I tell you

Go to the Word: Read Matthew 5:38–42.

You have heard that it was said

But I tell you

Go to the Word: Read Matthew 5:43–48.

You have heard that it was said

But I tell you

Do you notice how much more difficult it is to obey the commands that Jesus gives? Why is Jesus setting the standard so high?

In verse 20, He states what is really the issue. He is not concerned with His disciples simply following a law; Jesus is teaching that the standard they should be concerned with is true righteousness. That unless the disciples' righteousness is greater than that of the Pharisees, they cannot enter the kingdom of heaven.

Jesus doesn't just want our deeds; He wants all of us (Matthew 22:37–40). He wants His disciples to be different from the world because we are called to be citizens of the kingdom of heaven. And as citizens of heaven, Jesus wants us to live as though the kingdom were already here.

⟋⟋ ***Go to the Word:*** *Read Galatians 3:10-14.*

According to verses 10–11, can anyone be saved by works of the Law?

Write out verse 13 in your own words. What did Christ do for us?

Paul quotes Habakkuk 2:4 in verse 11. According to this quotation, how do the righteous live?

This righteousness that Jesus is talking about is not something that people can muster up inside themselves. In fact, this is truly the reason the Lord gave the Law. He wanted people to come to the conclusion that they could not accomplish this righteousness on their own. They would have to come to God in humility and depend on Him and His loving-kindness and grace in order to be saved.

PRAYER FOR FREEDOM

If you have come from a legalistic background or have a problem with legalistic thinking in any area of your life ("it has to be this way"), give that way of thinking over to God now. Focus on what Jesus did for us in breaking us free from being slaves to our sin so that we can strive for righteousness.

Day Three
ACCUSATION
Zechariah 3:1–5; 1 John 2:1–2; Romans 8:31–34

Who drew on my table? Who smeared toothpaste on the mirror? Who put mac 'n' cheese on the dog?!

In my house, the answer to these questions is usually the four- or five-year-old, and of course every child always blames the other. My two sensitive yet fiery middle children typically become enraged at each other for even the suggestion that they might be guilty of such heinous acts!

It's not fun to be accused, especially when you are innocent! Even our children recognize the discomfort of accusation. Why is being accused so uncomfortable? In part, it is the feeling of being judged along with the insecurity that judgment fosters, but I think especially in the case of my kids, it's the fear of consequences that puts us on edge.

~~ **Go to the Word:** *Read Zechariah 3:1–5.*

This vision given to Zechariah takes place after the kingdom of Judah has returned to Jerusalem and their ancestral land during the time of the Persian Empire.

Who is Joshua standing before?

Who is accusing the high priest Joshua?

According to verses 3 and 4, what was Satan's likely complaint about Joshua?

What did the angel of the Lord do?

At the climax of this scene in the throne room, Satan is pretty soundly rebuked by God. However, what is interesting is that Satan is not wrong in his accusations against Joshua. The angel of the Lord (possibly the preincarnate Jesus) is Joshua's advocate and takes care of him. He removes the dirty clothes and gives Joshua clean clothes fit for a celebration. This is what Jesus does for you and me—He is our advocate! When Satan points at us and calls us out, Jesus dismisses him, since the price has already been paid. When we have accepted salvation from Jesus, we have been made clean already. Jesus has paid our debt!

Recall a time when you were accused of something that you didn't do. Describe the situation and how it made you feel.

✐ Go to the Word: Read 1 John 2:1–2.

This passage talks about Jesus advocating on our behalf. Jesus is like our legal counsel before the Father. The idea is that our own sins, our own actions, condemn us before God. But Jesus, identified as "the righteous one," stands in for us as the record by which we are judged—His righteousness takes the place of our sins.

Jesus does this not just for us but for the whole world. How would you communicate 1 John 2:1–2 to someone who doesn't yet follow Christ?

~z~ **Go to the Word:** *Read Romans 8:31–34.*

There are some really amazing things in these verses. Paul asks a rhetorical question: "If God is for us, who is against us?" (verse 31). This statement is leading us to the conclusion that God has the final word. No one can oppose His assessment or judgment.

WHO JUSTIFIES US?

God is the One who changes our status before Him from indebted to free. He gives us the designation of having had our sins made right. We aren't fully righteous, but the Father declares us as such—based on merit that is given, not earned.

Once Jesus was raised to life, Paul writes that He now intercedes for us. He stands as our go-between before God. When our actions are called into question, He speaks for us.

PRAYER FOR FREEDOM

Write out Hebrews 7:25 in the space provided as a prayer of thanks for what Jesus is able to do. The words you write are the beautiful essence of the gospel of grace.

Day Four

GRACE AND CONSEQUENCES

Colossians 1:19–20; 2 Corinthians 5:15, 20–21

I have a confession to make. On occasion, I have been known to extend grace to my children out of parenting laziness and call it a learning experience! You know what I'm talking about, right? "You know, you deserve [insert consequence here], but instead Mommy is going to show you grace. Do you know what grace means?" And on we go from there.

While the logic is sound, I should most likely be doling out consequences, BUT it really is so important for our children to have a tangible example of grace. As humans, we have a much easier time understanding that which we can see with our own eyes and feel with our hearts. Many people think grace is the same as tolerance, but grace simply means "to be given unmerited favor." Sometimes what is needed more than consequences is an understanding of the grace that Jesus provides. And for those of us still trying to understand grace, Jesus has grace for us in that too.

▰▰▱ **Go to the Word:** *Read Colossians 1:19–20.*

What was God happy to have dwell in Him (Jesus)?

In your own words, what does it mean to have the Son of God dwell with us?

How is it possible for Jesus to reconcile everything to Himself and make peace?

✎ *Go to the Word:* Read 2 Corinthians 5:15.

Think about the amazing truth in this verse. Did any of us deserve this kind of treatment from Jesus? There is no way we could earn this treatment.

We received grace. *Grace* is defined as "God's unmerited favor toward humanity and especially his people, realized through the covenant and fulfilled through Jesus Christ."[2] *Unmerited* means there is nothing we did to earn it, and truly, there is nothing we could do to earn it. Jesus through His life and substitutionary death paved the way for us to be reconciled to God.

Jesus died so that we should no longer live for ourselves. How are you doing in this area? What else can you do to

be free of the compulsion to live for self instead of for Christ?

Go to the Word: Read 2 Corinthians 5:20.

What title are followers of Jesus given in this verse?

We are to plead with those who are far from God to be reconciled. Have you ever needed to be reconciled with someone and then the reconciliation actually happened? What was that experience like?

Verse 20 uses the word *plead*. We are to warn those who are outside the household of God to enjoy this reconciliation with God. An ambassador is someone who is chosen to represent a kingdom to another kingdom. Sometimes negotiations are successful and the two kingdoms can have peace. Other times, peace cannot be brokered and one nation must bear the consequences of an invading force.

Jesus desires that people would be reconciled to Him, even those who are opposed to Him and would count Him as their enemy.

So, the question naturally arises: How can we truly receive this reconciliation with God? If grace is unmerited favor, we cannot earn it, so how does this work?

Go to the Word: Read 2 Corinthians 5:21.

Who is the One who did not know sin?

What does this verse state we will become?

If we become the righteousness of God in Jesus, it's clear that there is no Law that is necessary for us to keep in order to win God's affections—none. For the one who would be a legalist, Jesus states that his righteousness must exceed that of the Pharisees and the scribes. There is only one way to receive that kind of righteousness and that's through Jesus.

PRAYER FOR FREEDOM

Thank God for His grace that frees us from the consequences of our own sin.

WEEK FOUR
Group Discussion

STARTER

Talk about a time when you made a quick judgment about someone and then later found out you were wrong. What made you snap to the judgment that you made so quickly? Or talk about when someone judged you incorrectly.

REVIEW

1. Is there an area of your life where you are fostering discontentment because of comparison?

2. How can we practically fulfill our calling as citizens of the kingdom of heaven?

3. In what way has Jesus traded your dirty clothes for clean clothes?

4. What is one thing about God's grace that you have a hard time comprehending or explaining to others?

5. How can we truly plead with people for reconciliation as ambassadors of the kingdom of heaven?

PRAYER FOR FREEDOM

Talk with one another about areas of your life in which you are very prone to make judgments or very aware of yourself being judged. Pray for God to release you from the emotional and mental patterns that keep you tied up in judgment.

FREEDOM FROM GUILT

It doesn't take long when we've done something wrong for guilt to kick in—it's human nature. Adam and Eve felt intense guilt and shame and hid from God after they had disobeyed His instructions; we often do the same thing. Our children don't have to be taught guilt either. They break something and sometimes run to hide—not just to escape punishment, but because they feel bad that they did something wrong.

As moms, guilt comes naturally. From the first moment we hold our babies, we begin to worry that we are doing it all wrong, that we're going to mess them up. Guilt can be an overwhelming force that erases any sign of freedom in us. How can we get back to freedom when guilt takes the wheel?

This week, we'll take a close look at sin, see what it looks like, and understand how to distinguish the source of our guilt. We'll be reminded that God wipes our records clean of our transgressions. We'll also dig into what the Bible has to say about works and learn how to find freedom from feeling like we need to overdo everything. And finally, we'll ask God to fill our places of lack and help us to find freedom instead of guilt!

Day One

A MORAL COMPASS AND GRACE
Romans 2–3

It had been a really rough day. Everyone was fighting with each other and on edge. I was downright annoyed and over it. You know the feeling—we've all been there. After putting everyone to bed in a frustrated, chaotic fury, I walked into the kitchen to have a cup of coffee and regroup for a few minutes. There on the counter was a note one of my daughters had written to her sister: "I'm so sorry I wouldn't be nice to you today. I love you so much and I'm so happy when you play with me! You are the best!" Then I flipped it over and on the back was this: "You are the person I love the most in the world (don't tell anyone else I said that!!!)."

I made sure to hide that note away for safekeeping (and to avoid anyone else's feelings in the house from getting hurt). I wanted to hold onto this reminder that the moral compass is there in my children, even when I question it at times.

God gave us a moral compass to help keep us on track— our conscience, which makes us aware of sin.

Go to the Word: *Read Romans 2:14–16.*

What do these verses tell you about the moral compass we have?

If we learned anything in week three of this study, it was that God loves sinners! He sent His Son to earth to spend time with sinners, to free sinners, and to die for sinners. He's all about sinners. And this is the best possible news for us, because we are all in that category!

Sin isn't just an action. It's not just something we do, like when we yell at our kids out of anger or covet our neighbor's new minivan (I never saw *that* day coming!).

Sin is actually a part of our DNA—it's our separation from God. Sin is what happens when we act out of alignment with our faith in Christ. Everyone does it: from the sweetest toddler to the most Mother Teresa–like lady who hands out peppermints to all the kids at church. (And yes, even Mother Teresa.)

Fill in the blank: Sin is _____ from God.

~ Go to the Word: Write out Romans 3:23.

All fall short. What that means is, while it's great to have a moral compass that steers us and reminds us to do the right thing, that's not going to be the thing that saves us. Following Jesus is not just about following all the rules. Our righteousness does not come from our obedience! Thinking we can achieve righteousness on our own, by following a certain set of rules or living out perfect lives, can lead us to being weighed down by expectations and guilt (when we don't meet those expectations). All fall short.

BUT JESUS. He is where our righteousness comes from (go back and check out Romans 3:22). He came to save us from ourselves, and His grace is the answer to all our sin, guilt, and shame.

He wiped our slates clean. He did it on the cross, and He's willing to do it each and every day. When we mess up yet again (and we will!), He will be there to pick up the pieces and make us new. The difficult part is that we still cling to our past and feel guilt from our sin. But what does God tell us about our sin, once we trust Him? He's forgotten it. He no longer sees it, thinks about it, or counts it against us (turn to Romans 4:7–8). If the sin is gone for God, why are you still clinging to it?

Go to the Word: Write out each verse below and let these promises of freedom from the guilt of your sin be a promise to you that God forgives you each time you go to Him!

Isaiah 38:17

Isaiah 43:25

Jeremiah 31:34

Micah 7:19

Guilt can be a good reminder for us to do something about our sin—to ask for forgiveness, to go make a broken relationship right, or to get an accountability partner, for example. (Or to write a super-sweet card to your sister.) But once we have confessed our sin to Christ, accepted His forgiveness, and done whatever we could do to repair any hurt we've caused, we can rest in the freedom God's grace and love have brought us. We can be free from guilt.

PRAYER FOR FREEDOM

What is something you are still clinging to? Is there guilt from sin in your past? Have you given it to God? Write out a prayer to God and give it over to Him if you haven't. If you have, ask God to remind you of His promises to you and how much He loves you! Be encouraged that you are free from guilt!

Day Two

YOU DON'T HAVE TO TRY SO HARD

James 2:14-26

I'm a doer. A people pleaser. A list maker. So, I spent a lot of my life thinking this was how I should approach God as well. I felt as if I needed a checklist to mark off—and I felt accomplished when I checked off the big things: go on a mission trip, CHECK, become a pastor's wife, CHECK, start a ministry, CHECK, write a Bible study, CHECK, CHECK, CHECK!

I was trying hard, probably a bit too hard most days. My faith was awfully shaky, because I was hoisting myself up on my own good deeds, sure that I could do it all on my own. Why shouldn't God be proud of me and all I've done? But I still just felt bad. Felt bad that I wasn't doing more. Felt bad that I wasn't doing it right. Felt bad that I wasn't pleasing Him in the right way.

And I had it wrong all along.

Pleasing God happens when we have faith and complete it with action. When we love Him and show Him that love with all our heart, soul, mind, and strength. Not by overdoing it and hoping He's pleased with a longer and longer list of all our good deeds—as if God's pleasure is fueled by our actions.

What do you want from your child? You want them to love you deeply and want to serve you (they could start with just cleaning their rooms for once!). You want them to serve because of how much they love and respect you, not out of fear or as a way of getting some reward. That's what God wants too. He wants our actions to come out of the faith and love we have for Him.

✐ **Go to the Word:** *James 2:14-26.*

What example does James give of what "dead faith" looks like (verses 15-16)?

What makes faith "useless" (verses 18-24)?

Sometimes we can get a little tripped up in the whole "faith without works is dead" idea. Are we supposed to just have faith? Are we supposed to work? Are we to do both? If you're like me, sometimes your head is spinning a bit; you just want to do the right thing. Let's take a deeper look so we can understand what James means here.

Compare verses 17 and 20. How does verse 20 help you understand what James means by "dead"?

Look at verse 26 and consider the imagery. What does this comparison tell us?

What does the concept of faith without works being dead mean to you?

Let's spend a little time looking at some other examples from Scripture and what they tell us about faith and works. Take some time reading through these. Write them out so you can understand them and look up words that may stump you.

Go to the Word: Read the following verses, then summarize what they say.

Ephesians 2:8–9

1 Corinthians 3:10–15

2 Corinthians 5:9–10

So, here's the deal. God wants your faith, not your to-do lists. Freedom comes with knowing that! It's beautiful and won-derful! He's not giving you a checklist or expecting a certain number of things from you. You really don't have to try so hard, friend. God is not laying guilt on you. He never has, and He never will. He's a giver of freedom and grace. You will desire to serve Him because you love Him; it's just one of the glorious perks that comes with being a follower of Christ.

PRAYER FOR FREEDOM

If it's still hard for you to grasp the idea that you don't have to try so hard to be pleasing to God in His eyes, then go back and read through the scriptures from this section again. Ask God to help you understand the message of freedom He has for you.

Day Three

FILL MY LACK
John 1:43–51; 2:1–12

If I'm being honest, I have to admit that many times I forget the importance of raising kids, and I think of the job as inconsequential. I get into this mode of thinking that it's something I do for a time in my life, or for a few hours a day. You see, I don't consider myself a "super mom," like many moms I know who can make organic meals, take their kids for ice cream on a school night, or really even have any of it all together. I'm too much of a perfectionist, which means if I can't do it perfectly, why try? I struggle to be the fun mom, the sporty mom, the best mom. So, I just give in to the guilt, the lies, and the belief that this mom thing is not for me. I start to feel unseen, unworthy, and unable to be more than just an okay-ish, part-time mom.

But that's not true of me, and it's not true of you either. Jesus sees us, knows us, and values us even when we feel unseen or unworthy. Let's look at a beautiful example of the way Jesus sees us.

*⌒ **Go to the Word:** Read John 1:43–51.*

What does Philip tell Nathanael he and the people had found?

What is Nathanael's response?

Nathanael was skeptical. Nazareth was a tiny town, not known for anything great. Why would the Messiah, the one who was to be king of the Jews, come from there?

But the man from Nazareth surprised Nathanael. He called Nathanael to follow Him by noting Nathanael's character, showing that He knew the man even before they had ever met. And Jesus said He saw Nathanael right where Philip had found him: "When you were under the fig tree, I saw you" (John 1:48).

Think about it: these poor people had no air conditioners, so everyone would spend a fair amount of time in the shade, finding a cool place. It's a good guess that anyone could be under a tree at any given time. But Jesus was specific, and this caught Nathanael's interest.

Nathanael realized that Jesus knew him. Jesus had seen him. Not just in the normal ways that humans know one another and see one another. Jesus had known Nathanael long before they ever laid eyes on each other. And Jesus had seen in his heart. Nathanael had been hiding out, in his unseen place. Maybe it was a place he had even gone to be alone or to sit and think. But Jesus had seen him there, and He knew him. And that was all Nathanael needed to follow Him.

When I read this story, it's as if Jesus is screaming at me, "I SEE YOU UNDER YOUR FIG TREE TOO!!!" I feel like I can hear Him reminding me, *I see you at the kitchen sink where you pray to me about the child you are battling with. I see you as you drive back and forth to school and sing songs of worship with your kids each morning. I see you as you scrub the dirty handprints off the walls and smile because you know this won't last forever. I see you when you lose your temper, but I know you love your family so much. I see you under your fig tree.*

Where do you feel unseen?

When have you felt that Jesus knew you?

Go to the Word: *Read John 2:1-12.*

What event was happening and what was the problem in this passage?

After Jesus called Philip and Nathanael, they attended a wedding, likely of a family friend. You probably know the story—even people who have never stepped foot inside a church have often heard of Jesus changing water into wine. In that culture, a wedding might have lasted for around a week—it would have been a big event, and the host would have been expected to provide enough food, wine, and resources for the duration. If a host came up short, that person risked becoming the laughingstock of the community for years to come.

Mary may have been near the place where the food and wine were prepared and heard they were running short; she wanted to do something to help her friends. So, she came to Jesus.

What did Mary say to Jesus and what did Jesus take her statement to mean?

Jesus said His hour had not yet come. What do you think He meant by that? (See also John 17:1.)

What could you guess about Mary's relationship with and experience of Jesus that would cause her to go to Him for help in this situation?

Mary saw a place of lacking, and asked Jesus to step in and fill it. We might just see in this story a mother asking her son for help. But what we can also see is that Mary trusted Jesus. She did not know what He would do. But she knew who He was. She knew He was the Son of God. "Do whatever he tells you," she said, and she completely trusted that whatever He said would be good (John 2:5).

Note—you may be wondering why people couldn't just drink water. First, it was a wedding, and wine was a symbol of celebration. But second, the water wasn't drinkable by itself. They didn't have clean water running from a tap like we do today. They had to have wine because it purified the water enough to drink (but it was heavily diluted, around four parts water to one part wine). So, the wine was a necessity, because they literally had run out of anything safe to drink. They needed someone to fill their jars.

Consider where you are feeling overwhelming lack. Where do you feel you aren't enough? Where do you need Jesus to come in and perform some miracies? To bring joy out of nothing?

Many times, our lack leads to feelings of guilt and shame, but Jesus wants to fill us up. He wants us to be whole so He can keep the party going and He can be praised and glorified through us!

PRAYER FOR FREEDOM

As you prepare to pray, think about how you would complete this sentence: I feel I am lacking because of _____.

Ask God to provide what you lack.

Day Four

HE CHOSE YOU

John 15:16; 2 Corinthians 10:1–5

I will never forget the first time I lost it and yelled at my kids. *Oh! This is what motherhood is really like!* I thought, after I had screamed at my kids to behave like civilized human beings and put their shoes away. I wish I could say that was the last time I yelled at my kids or did something else I later regretted. I struggle every day with nagging thoughts:

I should have handled that situation differently.

I should have spoken kinder or softer.

I shouldn't have blown up over that homework.

I should have actually cooked dinner instead of getting pizza ... again.

I should get up and go spend time with my husband, but I'd rather lie here in bed eating chocolate.[1]

Mom guilt is real, and it can overwhelm us. It's not something new or something that just a few of us battle with. Every time I talk to a mom about guilt, the answer is always a resounding "Yes, I struggle with this!" But the truth of the matter is this: *God chose you.* Fill in the blanks below with the name of your child or names of your children. Then repeat that sentence again and again.

God chose me to be _____**'s mom.**

God chose me to be _____**'s mom.**

God chose me to be _____**'s mom.**

God chose me to be _____**'s mom.**

Go to the Word: *Read John 15:16.*

Many times, I think we forget that God created us. We were made to worship Him—not the other way around. This scripture gives us a heaping dose of perspective. He chose us. He made us. He placed us right where we are to produce fruit—good things that will come from the fact that we are connected to Him.

But we are selfish people. We let ourselves get wrapped up in our own lives, and we choose guilt over freedom, because guilt is easier. Let's consider some ways that guilt has been the easy way out for you. Complete the following sentences with the actions or attitudes or events that are happening right now, or that have happened in the past, that have made you feel guilty.

I have felt guilty because _____.
I have felt guilty because _____.
I have felt guilty because _____.

The list could probably go on and on. But these are lies, and we are going to fight these lies with the truth of the Word of God. If you have received the forgiveness of Christ, your sin is gone. If you have tried your best to repair hurt relationships, then it's time to stop feeling guilty and move on toward being the person God has made you to be.

Maybe your guilt is from sin. Maybe your guilt is from not spending time with your kids. Maybe your guilt is from being angry or frustrated. No matter what, don't let guilt stop you from producing fruit.

⌁ **Go to the Word:** *Write out 2 Corinthians 10:1–5.*

When thinking about guilt, how could we wage war against it in a way that is different from what the world does?

When your guilty thoughts slip in, call them out and replace them with truth. We can take these thoughts captive and go to battle against them, because Jesus wants to set us free from our guilt. He's already set you free from your sin—of course He wants to set your mind free of the guilt you cling to! Imagine the freedom you would feel as a woman, wife, and mother if you walked through life guilt-free!

Do your homework: What is your place of guilt? Ask God to reveal those places to you, and then go to the Word and find scripture to fight against any guilt or shame that the enemy is holding over your head. The Word of God is a weapon that we can take to battle against our enemies, and guilt is an ugly, nasty enemy! Face it with verses like these:

Jeremiah 1:5
John 1:12
Romans 6:6

Romans 8:37
Romans 15:7
1 Corinthians 6:17
2 Corinthians 5:17
Galatians 2:20
Colossians 3:1–3
2 Timothy 1:7
1 Peter 2:9
1 John 3:1–2

PRAYER FOR FREEDOM

As you pray today, listen to how God is challenging you to walk in freedom. Focus on how to give Him glory instead of sinking into your guilt. Write down these challenges for yourself:

Today I will focus on _____ **instead of**
_____.

Today I will focus on _____ **instead of**
_____.

WEEK FIVE

Group Discussion

STARTER

Talk about a time this past week or so when you felt "mommy guilt." What happened? What did you do about that feeling?

REVIEW

1. How is striving to do things on our own connected to our struggle with guilt?

2. Discuss what you learned about the idea that faith without works is dead. What does this mean? Do you find yourself trying too hard or overcompensating for some sort of guilt you battle? How does this hold you back?

3. What did you learn from the story of Jesus turning water to wine? What stood out to you? How does this help remind you that God can fill your lack?

4. Read 2 Corinthians 10:5. How can you take guilty thoughts captive? What has helped you as you've been challenging yourself to walk in freedom instead of letting guilt weigh you down?

5. Talk about the difference between healthy, godly ways of feeling guilt (guilt that leads to conviction and repentance—see 2 Corinthians 7:10) and unhealthy, harmful ways of holding on to guilt.

PRAYER FOR FREEDOM

Using scraps of paper, let each person write a few words or draw an image of something that represents a stubborn bit of guilt that they have trouble letting go of completely. Form a circle, and let each person pass her scrap to the person on the left. Then as you pray together, asking God to provide what you lack and arm you well for waging war with guilt, tear up the scraps into tiny pieces.

FREEDOM FROM THE WORLD

"You're finally moving to a bigger place, right?" This was the question we heard over and over again when we found out we were pregnant with our fourth daughter. We had made our little two-bedroom, one-bath house work so far, and with rent prices what they were, we wanted to wait as long as possible before we had to pay even more money!

Owning our own home, having the newest minivan and the trendiest clothes—these are some of the things the world tells us we must have to be happy and fulfilled. We are told we deserve them. We need them.

The truth is that, rather than fulfilling us and giving us more freedom, these things can actually bring bondage. Perhaps it's a mortgage or car payment we can't afford, or the worry of living up to some image we think is expected of us; all these concerns can keep us from being all that God designed us to be. Debt can keep us from being generous, and self-focus can deter us from seeing what others need.

This week, we set ourselves apart. We detach ourselves from the lies the world throws at us. We speak truth in the face of lies. We choose freedom!

Day One

IN THE WORLD, NOT OF THE WORLD

2 Corinthians 5:17; Galatians 5:17–26; John 17:13–19

How long has it been since you saw Disney's *The Little Mermaid*? Depending on your kids' ages (or just your own movie collection), it may be playing right now in the background somewhere as you read this. The story of *The Little Mermaid* is about a mermaid (of course) who wants to live beyond her own world and experience life as a surface dweller. It's a classic story of someone who feels completely separated from the one they love by their place in the world.

Now for some of you, just the mention of this story will bring the songs from the film to mind. In fact, they will now be stuck in your head all day (you're welcome). The most iconic song is "Part of Your World." Ariel shares her innermost longing to join the two-legged folks on the surface. She expresses the ache of feeling separated from who she wants to be because of, well, a lack of legs.

The original story about the little mermaid was written by Hans Christian Andersen, a Danish storyteller whose stories have inspired many adaptations (including another Disney smash hit about a queen with a peculiar ice obsession). In nineteenth-century Denmark, Andersen had developed a major crush on a Russian ballerina who had come to perform in Copenhagen. However, he felt he could never be with her, because she was so famous and beautiful. The original fairy tale ends in tragedy when the mermaid and the prince realize they can never be truly together because they are from two very different worlds. The mermaid leaps to the sea and turns to sea-foam. That's a little darker, and maybe more real, than the Disney version for sure!

These stories about being from two different worlds relate to our stories of meeting and knowing Jesus. Before we knew Jesus, we were like anyone else in this world. We were in darkness, and we liked the darkness. In fact, we would not have known the light even if we saw it (John 1). But then Jesus brought the light, His light, into the world, into our lives, and that changed us.

We all have unique stories of how the Lord has drawn us to Himself. At some point, we realize our condition, and we confess and repent of our sin. Jesus, in His grace, gives us His righteousness and saves us from ourselves. We become something new. We are no longer our former selves; we no longer fit in the world of darkness.

Go to the Word: **2 Corinthians 5:17.**

What's your favorite part about this verse?

Because we are not who we once were, we are not the same. We don't do the things we did when we were our "old selves." Our priorities are different. Our goals are changing to be our Master's goals. We are now a part of *His* world, and it is where we truly belong.

Go to the Word: **Galatians 5:17–26.**

This passage on the fruit of the Spirit should be familiar, but in this section, what are the fruit of the flesh?

Some of the things on this list would be obvious, but what are some things on the list of acts of the flesh that surprise you?

Because of our place in Jesus, we are now people of the Spirit, not the flesh. We are now fit for living in the kingdom of heaven, and Jesus is making us more like citizens of that kingdom daily. The fruit of the flesh are being displaced by the fruit of the Spirit.

Go to the Word: John 17:13-19.

Jesus prayed this prayer for His followers, His friends. He knew He was going to be on the way to the cross soon. Even though Jesus was going to suffer and die in this world, because He was not of this world (see verse 14), He prayed for His followers.

In your own words, from verse 15, what did Jesus ask the Father to do?

If we have been made into a new creation and we are not of the world, we are free from the worries and expectations and pressures that are on those who are of the world. The world as it is now is slowly passing away (1 John 2:17), and our Father does not want us to be tied to the same fate. Separation from the world is an important key to our survival.

Jesus asked His Father to separate out His disciples from the world in truth. According to John 17:17, how could this happen?

Are you still living like you belong in this world? Even after being set apart, do you continue to look like you are part of this world? Though we live here for now, we are no longer from here. We are citizens of another world.

Ask your heart this question: What is it in this world that is so difficult to let go of?

PRAYER FOR FREEDOM

Look again at the words of Jesus' prayer in John 17, and use His words as your prayer today. Ask God to protect you and to sanctify you.

Freedom

Day Two
ETERNAL PERSPECTIVE
2 Kings 6:15–17; Ephesians 6:10–19

Living in this world can get busy and hectic. There are so many things around us that compete for our attention. Beyond just normal life with kids and school, sporting events and dance class, playdates and coffee chats, errands and various deadlines, there is even more. As Christian mamas, we want to pursue Jesus in our relationships and be examples to our littles. Sometimes, it's just tough to be excited for heaven and the Lord's promises while figuring out how to get play clay out of the universal remote.

We know that this world is not all there is. In the Scriptures, not only are we told of the reality of heaven and the spiritual realm, but we are taught that the "other side" is more accessible than our eyes would tell us. But even though God is close to us, have you ever been in a situation where you could not see what He was doing? There's a story like that from the life of the prophet Elisha.

Go to the Word: 2 Kings 6:15–17.

In this passage, Elisha the prophet was in the midst of a siege. Who warned Elisha of the army besieging the city?

In verse 16, what was the reason Elisha stated that his servant should not be afraid?

There are times in life when the Lord truly must open our eyes to what He is doing or we will miss it. What this passage teaches is that the reality of the army of chariots and horses and fire was never up for debate. The servant simply did not perceive the spiritual reality around him. His eyes had to be opened.

Go to the Word: Ephesians 6:10–19.

Verse 11 states that we need the armor of God to stand against the devil, our accuser and enemy. What does verse 12 say we are *not* fighting against?

What does verse 12 state we *are* fighting against?

Since the battle is with spiritual forces, it would make sense that our armor is also spiritual. List the elements of the armor of God.

Most of the armor would be considered defensive pieces. What is the weapon for offense that we have?

Notice there are two actions required of us in verse 18. What are they?

Prayer is one of those forgotten elements in our spiritual battle. It is often overlooked in its importance. The reality is, someone with a proper eternal perspective is going to see prayer as important and vital. Prayer makes us aware of our spiritual reality and leads us to engage with the supernatural world. We worship and follow a supernatural God who does supernatural things. Prayer is anticipation and expectation of the supernatural becoming our reality.

Reminder: How often does verse 18 say we should pray?

This spiritual battle that we are warned of is not a onetime skirmish. This fight is a daily fight. And because this battle is invisible to our eyes, it can be very easy to lose focus and perspective.

Write out verse 13 as a challenge to yourself.

Are you ready to take your stand every day? This is the perspective that we must maintain.

PRAYER FOR FREEDOM

Ask God to open your eyes, just like He opened the eyes of Elisha's servant. Ask Him to show you that He has provided you with everything you need to take a stand against the enemy and his schemes.

Day Three
NOT OUR HOME
Exodus 12:1–11; 2 Corinthians 5:1–7; John 14:1–7

It's easy to get caught up in our current dwellings. There are a number of TV series, books, podcasts, and magazines focused on home management and decoration. People put a lot of time and effort into making their spaces perfect, or at least perfect for now. Between Hobby Lobby, Target, and IKEA, it's a wonder we have time or energy for anything else.

Now, don't misunderstand, we all like to have a clean, well-lit, tastefully decorated space for our family, and it's a pleasure to offer the same for our friends and neighbors. But let's be honest, some of the attention to our homes is not based on serving others.

For the people of Israel, home for years had been in a state of oppression. They could not own very much because they were slaves—forced to work for a harsh ruler who had no compassion for them. The story of Israel's deliverance from slavery is recorded in Exodus. After a series of nine plagues, Pharaoh's heart was still hardened to the request to let the people of Israel go into the desert to worship Yahweh—God.

But then, God decided the time had come. He gave the Israelites detailed instructions on how to prepare for the first Passover.

Go to the Word: *Read Exodus 12:1–11.*

In verse 11, God told Moses and Aaron to make sure the people were prepared to leave—He was planning on delivering them out of slavery very soon.

What if you were told that the very next day you would be leaving your home and not coming back? What would you pack?

What if you only could fill the trunk of your car? How does that change your answer?

It's so easy to get caught up in the lives we build. Even though the Israelites were slaves, it was hard for them to leave everything familiar behind and begin a journey into uncertainty.

The Lord was forcing His people to have a perspective that looked beyond their current dwelling to a promised, future dwelling. Would they trust Him to lead them there? Would they take Yahweh up on this offer to provide a place for them? Passover allowed them a chance to reset their perspective.

Go to the Word: Read 2 Corinthians 5:1–7.

What are the two dwellings called in verses 1 and 2?

Other than dwellings, what other word picture is used in verses 1–7?

According to verse 5, what is the down payment on our heavenly dwelling?

Paul's perspective in this letter is that death means just going away from the bodies we now have and into an eternal dwelling. He does not see death as final (for those who believe in Christ), but as a step toward completing our earthly race and being "swallowed up by life" that we find in God (verse 4).

⌁ Go to the Word: Read John 14:1–4.

In this passage, Jesus has just completed the last meal He will enjoy on earth, and Judas, His betrayer, has left the group. The eleven remaining disciples are with Jesus for a final teaching and prayer.

How many dwelling places are there in the Father's house?

What does Jesus promise to do?

The promise in these verses is not just for the disciples sitting with Jesus but for us as well. Once our Lord returns and receives us, we will be with Him. That will be our status.

*~ **Go to the Word:** Read John 14:6-7.*

Jesus told them that they knew the way to where He was going. But Thomas asked, "How can we know the way?" (verse 5).

What was Jesus' answer?

There is only one way to get to the heavenly dwelling, and that is through Jesus. He holds all the keys to the kingdom of heaven. While we wait in this tent, let us encourage one another to maintain a proper perspective on our permanent dwelling and not to make our earthly tent too permanent in our hearts. No one wants to camp forever!

PRAYER FOR FREEDOM

Ask God to help you do what is needed to prepare for your heavenly dwelling and to keep you focused on what's important.

Day Four

DEATH ISN'T THE END

Luke 16:19–31; Matthew 7:21–23; Philippians 1:20–21

Death is not easy to talk about in our culture. There is a finality to death that makes people uncomfortable. In some other cultures, death is regarded as a part of life and is discussed more naturally. One factor that might contribute to the awkwardness around death is that many people say they don't believe in the supernatural—they don't believe in life after death. So, for them, death is very much the end.

For those of us who are followers of Jesus, death is not the end, but a part of the plan that the Lord has for us.

➤ **Go to the Word:** *Read Luke 16:19–31.*

Jesus once told a parable about two men. One man was a beggar named Lazarus. The other was a rich unnamed man.

This is the only parable in which Jesus gives a name to a character. Why do you think Jesus mentions the name of the beggar but not the rich man?

How would you explain the reasons the rich man ended up in torment while the poor man was carried away by the angels?

✒ Go to the Word: *Read Matthew 7:21-23.*

What do these verses tell you about who will or will not enter the kingdom of heaven?

✒ Go to the Word: *Read Philippians 1:20-21.*

To live is Christ. To die is gain. The word for *gain* in Greek is an accounting term. It means that, when all the columns are tallied, we are in the black. There is a profit. So, when we die, it is actually a profit to us. This also means that, at the moment, while we live, we are not as full or as rich as we one day will be.

Do you really believe that? If so, how do you show that you believe that what we will have and experience after death will be gain for us?

If we do believe that this is true, as we look forward to our final destination, then death should not be a taboo subject, at least not with believers.

One question moms ask from time to time is, how do we talk with our little ones about death?

This is a very sensitive subject for some children, and we would not attempt to give specific counsel or recommendations without knowing a child's particular experience. But to speak generally, this is where we can begin to break the taboo concerning the discussion of death. Two simple statements: (1) everyone dies; and (2) everyone who accepts Jesus as Savior has a promised place to go. The more these facts become commonplace and the more we discuss these simple truths in a safe context, the less scary death will become for our children. Let Jesus be the hero in our homes, and make heaven a familiar subject—the hope of eternal freedom!

Read through these verses and draw out from them the hopeful message of our life eternal: 1 Peter 1:3–5; Philippians 3:20; Colossians 1:5.

PRAYER FOR FREEDOM

Bring any fears you might have about death to God. Become like a child and ask the questions you want to ask. Search Scripture to find out what you want to know. Ask God to help the hope of eternal life to bring you freedom every day.

Group Discussion

STARTER

When you were a child, what did you imagine heaven would be like? What kinds of conversations have you had with your children (if they are old enough) about life after death?

REVIEW

1. What in this world do you find difficult to let go of?

2. In what ways does being a follower of Christ make you different from other people? How does it change your perspective?

3. Do you often "desire to put on your heavenly dwelling," or do you have a hard time with the idea of leaving your earthly tent? Explain why you feel the way you do right now, and talk about whether your feelings about this have been different at other points in your life.

4. How can we incorporate the hope of heaven into our daily conversations?

5. How can making the hope of heaven a daily reality bring us freedom?

PRAYER FOR FREEDOM

As you close your study of freedom together, let each person share one way they feel they have been able to become more free through this study. Pray for one another, asking God to help you encourage everyone in the group to keep finding ways to let go of what is holding you back and embrace Christ instead.

Room to Reflect

LEADER GUIDE

Hello, Leaders!

Thank you for investing in the lives of the women around you! Whether this is your first time leading a Bible study or you've led many groups before, we appreciate the time and sacrifice you make for your group. We want to come alongside you and help you feel prepared to lead. Here you will find a starting-off point to help you prepare for your meeting times.

The group discussions can range from about 30-45 minutes if you are meeting in person. Below you will find a suggested outline for your group time, but feel free to tailor your time together to fit your needs.

GETTING STARTED TIPS

PRAY!!

As you are preparing to lead your group, prayer is key!! Spend time each week praying for the ladies in your group and praying that God will lead and direct your time.

FIND A LOCATION

Decide what works best for your group. Meeting at someone's house? At a coffee shop? In a local park? At a church? Online? Get some feedback. If the women in your group don't have the transportation, means, or the time to meet up somewhere—consider hosting an online Facebook group. We provide tips for how to do this at thrivemoms.com/community. If you have a really large group and can meet at your church, consider providing childcare.

PLAN AND PREPARE

Be very familiar with your material! Read through the material and make notes before your discussion time so you can make sure your time together flows smoothly.

FOLLOW UP

Take time during the week to follow up with the women in your group and check in on how they are doing. Remind them about meeting times, and encourage engagement within your group.

GROUP LEADING TIPS

BEFORE YOU MEET

Take some time to go through the week of material and make notes on anything that you may need to clarify deeper with your group. As a leader, you need to be prepared, so make sure you have answered every question, filled in every blank, and read all of the content. Go through all of the group discussion questions, answering each one and having questions picked out that you think will be good for your group. You can also use space on the discussion pages or the Room to Reflect pages to add questions or thoughts of your own.

Keep your mind and heart open to how the Lord leads your group. You may have someone come with a question, concern, or need that may take more time than you are prepared for. Your group time may not always look the way you think, so leave room for growth. Remember that your group members are getting into the material on their own too.

PREPARE

Helping to set a comfortable and inviting atmosphere for your group is a great way to start your meeting time each week.

This may be the only time during the week your women have away from their kids or (if kids are at the location) one of the few chances they have to partake in focused adult conversations that aren't all about their children or their work stress. You want them to walk in and feel a sense of peace and rest. Being a thoughtful host makes a huge difference in the atmosphere of your group and in your ability to connect with one another and the content.

Here are a few ways you can prepare for your group time:

- Pray over the room and each person attending.
- Minimize any distractions (remove sight and sound clutter as much as possible) and create a comfortable environment, with seating available for everyone. Your group will struggle to engage if they are uncomfortable and distracted.
- If you are hosting online—post ahead of time, welcoming them. Make sure your live video setup is comfortable and inviting, with clear sound and enough light.

WELCOME (10 Minutes)

As your group arrives, take some time to welcome each person and catch up briefly on what's happening in people's lives. Make any introductions or announcements you need to here. If drinks or snacks are available, invite everyone to get those before they find their seats.

DISCUSSION (20–30 Minutes)

Use the Starter question, if you wish, to begin the conversation. Sometimes, especially in groups where the members don't know one another well, it can be helpful to have a chance to talk about more everyday issues before diving into the spiritual discussion.

After a few people have responded to the Starter, move into the Review of the week's study by discussing the provided questions. If you are in the second week of the study or any week past that, it might also be helpful for you to briefly summarize the main points of the previous session (especially if some members haven't been able to make it to every meeting).

Allow people to share anything that stood out to them and to ask questions about any parts of the session they didn't understand. If you can, take notes about any specific needs or issues your group members mention so you can pray for those later.

PRAYER (5–10 Minutes)

After you complete your discussion time, build prayer into each group session. Prayer prompts are provided, or you may wish to spend some time going around and praying for the specific needs of your group members. Note pages are provided at the end of each session so people can jot down reminders of any needs they may want to continue praying over during the week. Check in with your women throughout the week and pray for them daily!

NOTES

WEEK ONE: WHAT IS FREEDOM IN CHRIST?

1. David Guzik, "Galatians 3—The Christian, Law, and Living by Faith," Enduring Word, 2018, accessed May 26, 2019, https://enduringword.com/bible-commentary/galatians-3/.

2. *Aladdin*, directed by Ron Clements and John Musker (Burbank, CA: Walt Disney, 1992).

3. *Black Panther*, directed by Ryan Coogler (Burbank, CA: Walt Disney, 2018).

4. *Strong's Concordance*, s.v. "doulos," Bible Hub, accessed May 26, 2019, https://biblehub.com/greek/1401.htm.

5. Francis Chan, *Forgotten God: Reversing Our Tragic Neglect of the Holy Spirit* (Colorado Springs: David C Cook, 2009), 16–17.

WEEK THREE: FREEDOM FROM EXPECTATION

1. Craig S. Keener, *The IVP Bible Background Commentary New Testament* (Downers Grove, IL: InterVarsity, 2014), 228–29.

WEEK FOUR: FREEDOM FROM JUDGMENT

1. Martin H. Manser, *Dictionary of Bible Themes: The Accessible and Comprehensive Tool for Topical Studies* (London: Martin Manser, 2009).

2. Allen C. Myers, ed., *The Eerdmans Bible Dictionary* (Grand Rapids, MI: Eerdmans, 1987), 437.

WEEK FIVE: FREEDOM FROM GUILT

1. Slightly revised from Kara-Kae James, *Mom Up: Thriving with Grace in the Chaos of Motherhood* (Colorado Springs: David C Cook, 2019), 161.

ABOUT THE AUTHORS

Kara-Kae James is a writer and encourager, passionate about seeing women's lives changed and impacted through the gospel. She is the founder and executive director of Thrive Moms, a ministry dedicated to seeing moms step out of survival mode and into the thriving, abundant life that God calls them to. She is also the author of the book *Mom Up: Thriving with Grace in the Chaos of Motherhood*.

Kara-Kae is married to her husband, Brook, and is a mom to four. She works daily to encourage women to reach their potential as moms and as daughters of Christ. She loves pouring into moms because she knows firsthand that many are struggling and in desperate need of a reminder that God loves us, and we are doing His holy work.

Ali Pedersen is a writer and pastor's wife who has a heart for bringing people together. She is the community director of Thrive Moms and works with women to find fellowship right where they are.

Ali is married to her husband, Nicolai, and is a mom to four girls. She spends her days creating resources for women, homeschooling her kiddos, and baking lots of cookies. She enjoys fostering community among women and creating deep relationships for the sake of the kingdom.

TM

EMPOWERING IMPERFECT MOMS WITH GOD'S PERFECT GRACE.

We invite you to join the Thrive Moms' Community—
a community of real women who are stepping out of
survival mode and into thriving, abundant life with Christ.
We focus on community, intentionality as moms,
finding our rest in the Lord, and embracing the
wonderfully chaotic moments of everyday life.
We continue to push each other deeper into God's Word
and know that we are better when we stand together.

JOIN US AT **THRIVEMOMS.COM** AND
DOWNLOAD THE **THRIVE MOMS APP**.

@thrivemoms

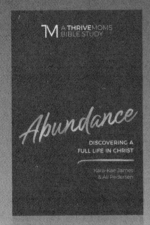

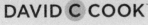